3 WOMEN

BY
KATY BRAND

║SAMUEL FRENCH║

samuelfrench.co.uk

3WOMEN

Premiered at the Trafalgar Studios on 18 May 2018

CAST
In order of appearance

SUZANNE	Debbie Chazen
WAITER	Oliver Greenall
ELEANOR	Anita Dobson
LAURIE	Maisie Richardson-Sellers

CREATIVES

Director	Michael Yale
Producer / Creative Director	Eilene Davidson
Marketing and PR Director	Susanna Gulliford
Assistant Producer	Sarah Reed
Set and Costume Designer	Zahra Mansouri
Lighting Designer	Nic Farman
Casting Director	Ellie Collyer-Bristow CDG

Trafalgar
Studios

'A new venue that's changing the shape of the West End.' *The Times*

Trafalgar Studios opened on 26th May 2004 and, with two auditoria under a single roof, was the first theatre of its kind in the heart of London's West End.

In 2017, theatre entrepreneurs Sir Howard Panter and Dame Rosemary Squire acquired Trafalgar Studios as the flagship for a new venture that combines live entertainment with distinctive cultural buildings, original content and live-streaming. They will continue to build on the Trafalgar Studios' reputation for fresh and challenging work which has included Lee Evans and Jason Isaacs in the 50th Anniversary production of Harold Pinter's *The Dumb Waiter*; the hit comedy *Elling*, starring John Simm and Adrian Bower; *Riflemind* directed by Philip Seymour Hoffman; *Entertaining Mr Sloane*, starring Imelda Staunton and Mathew Horne; *The Mountaintop* and *Othello* starring Lenny Henry, and James McAvoy in Jamie Lloyd's ground breaking production of *Macbeth*, which launched the much anticipated Trafalgar Transformed seasons. These featured Simon Russell Beale and John Simm in *The Hothouse*; *The Pride* starring Hayley Atwell; Martin Freeman as *Richard III*; *East is East*, with Jane Horrocks, and T*he Ruling Class*. The critically acclaimed Golem and Robert Icke's stunning production of *Oresteia* followed. In 2016 Studio 1 was home to the hugely successful razor-sharp comedy *The Spoils*, written by and starring Jesse Eisenberg, and Sam Shepard's American classic *Buried Child*, starring Ed Harris. In 2017, Studio 1 welcomed Emmy Award winner Stockard Channing in Alexi Kaye Campbell's *Apologia*, the critically acclaimed new British musical *The Grinning Man* and Orlando Bloom in Tracy Letts' *Killer Joe*.

Trafalgar Studios' second space, Studio 2 presents inspiring, thoughul and adventurous new work from the best national and international companies. Offering a uniquely intimate theatre experience in the heart of the West End, this 100 seat studio promotes new writing and celebrates fresh talent.

Cyprus, a political thriller by Peter Arnott from Mull Theatre launched the first season of work. Other highlights have included Horla's new adaptation of Dickens' *A Christmas Carol*; Michael Morpurgo's *Private*

Peaceful; Neil LaBute's *Bash*; *Lifecoach*, starring Phil Jupitus; *The Quiz*, performed by David Bradley; *Touched*, performed by Sadie Frost; and *New Boy*, starring Nicholas Hoult.

In 2013 the Donmar Warehouse produced a season of plays at Trafalgar Studios, *The Promise*, *The Dance of Death* and *The Silence of the Sea*, *Left Hand* with Imogen Stubbs and the smash-hit comedy *The Play That Goes Wrong* which went on to take the West End by storm. Since then, productions have included *Dessa Rose*, with Cynthia Erivo; *Boa*, with Harriet Walter; *Bomber's Moon*, with James Bolam; *As Is*; *Rotterdam*; *BU21*; *Speech and Debate*; *Disco Pigs*; *Le Grand Mort*, with Julian Clary; a season from the King's Head Theatre, which included the Olivier-nominated opera *La Bohème* and *Rasheeda Speaking*, with Elizabeth Berrington and Tanya Moodie.

Trafalgar Studio 2 has been made possible by a generous donation from Christina Smith.

CAST

DEBBIE CHAZEN
Suzanne

Debbie Chazen's numerous theatre credits include: *The Girls* (Phoenix Theatre/UK Tour), for which the female cast were Olivier Award-nominated as a collective, for Best Actress in a Musical; *A Lovely Sunday for Creve Coeur* (Coronet Print Room); *Listen, We're Family* (Wilton's Music Hall); *The Duck House* (Vaudeville Theatre); *A Little Hotel on the Side* (Theatre Royal, Bath); *Open Court: The President Has Come to See You, Mint, Untitled Matriarch Play* and *In Basildon* (Royal Court); *Calendar Girls* (Noël Coward Theatre/UK Tour); *The Girlfriend Experience* (Royal Court/Young Vic/Plymouth); *Cinderella* (Old Vic); *The Cherry Orchard* (Sheffield Crucible); *Dick Whittington* (Barbican); *Crooked* (Bush Theatre); *A Prayer for Owen Meaney* and *Mother Clap's Molly House* (National Theatre & West End); *A Midsummer Night's Dream* (Noël Coward Theatre); and *The Rise and Fall of Little Voice* (Salisbury Playhouse).

Her work for television includes: *Holby City, The Last Kingdom, Dead Pixels, Agatha Raisin, You, Me and the Apocalypse, Ambassadors, Asylum, Sherlock, Trollied, The Spa, Coronation Street, Doctor Who, Tittybangbang, This Is Jinsy, White Van Man, Doctors* (nominated for Villain of the Year – Soap Awards 2010 for twelve episodes as Sissy Juggins), *We Are Klang, Psychoville, The Smoking Room, Nicholas Nickleby, Mine All Mine, Murder in Suburbia, Doc Martin, Midsomer Murders, Gimme Gimme Gimme, Lucy Sullivan Is Getting Married, Tess of the D'Urbervilles, A Christmas Carol* and *The Lakes.* Film credits include: Mike Leigh's *Topsy Turvy, Suzie Gold, Tooth*, Anton Chekhov's *The Duel* and most recently *Red Joan*, directed by Trevor Nunn.

OLIVER GREENALL
Waiter

Oliver Greenall is an actor, writer and director. He was born in Scotland and trained at PACE Youth Theatre. During his final year of school, he was scouted by the model agency Models 1 and worked on various international campaigns for some of the largest fashion houses in the world. He went on to study at Glasgow University and received a BA in film-making and screenwriting at UWS. In 2015, he wrote and directed his first short film, *Directions*, which was screened at festivals all around the world, including the London Short Film Festival in 2017. Television credits include: series regular Jordan Whitehead in ITV's *The Loch*, and *Armchair Detectives* for BBC Television. Oliver will be making his West End debut at the Trafalgar Studios in *3Women*.

ANITA DOBSON
Eleanor

Anita Dobson is an Olivier Award nominated and well-loved television, theatre and fi lm actress. Anita's many stage appearances include *Budgie* (Cambridge Theatre); *Three Sisters* (Royal Court); *Le Bourgeois Gentilhomme* (National Theatre); *Kvetch* (Garrick Theatre); *My Lovely... Shayna Maidel* (The Ambassadors Theatre); *Charley's Aunt* (Aldwych Theatre); *The Pajama Game* (Victoria Palace Theatre); *The Vagina Monologues* (Arts Theatre/UK Tour); *The Island of Slaves* (Lyric, Hammersmith); *Frozen* (National Theatre), for which she was nominated for an Olivier Award, Evening Standard, and London Critics' Circle Theatre Award; *Chicago* (Adelphi Theatre); *Thoroughly Modern Millie* (Shaftesbury Theatre); *Hamlet* (New Ambassadors Theatre/UK Tour); *Hello Dolly* (Theatre Royal Lincoln/ UK Tour); Kurt Weill's opera *The Silver Lake* (Wexford Festival); *Calendar Girls* (Noël Coward Theatre); *Two Sisters* (Eastbourne and Brighton); *Sleeping Beauty* (Richmond Theatre); *Strictly Come Dancing Live!*; *Bette and Joan* (Arts Theatre); *The Merry Wives of Windsor* (RSC), Steven Berkoff's production of *Oedipus* (Edinburgh Festival at the Pleasance Grand.); *Carnival of the Animals*; *Crush – A Girl's Own Musical*; *Follies* (Royal Albert Hall); *She Stoops to Conquer* (Theatre Royal, Bath); *Wicked* (Apollo Victoria Theatre) and most recently *The Shadow Factory* (Nuffield, Southampton). As Angie Watts in *EastEnders*, Anita Dobson was one of the most popular characters on television, winning her the PYE award for Television Personality of the Year, The Daily Mirror's Actress of the Year and the TV Times Actress of the Year Award, voted by the readers.

Other television includes: *Leave Him to Heaven, Nanny, The House of Lurking Death, Up the Elephant and Round the Castle, Split Ends, The World of Eddie Weary, Red Dwarf, Rab C. Nesbitt, Smokescreen, I'll Be Watching You, Dangerfield, The Famous Five, Highlander, Get Well Soon, Junk, Sunburn, The Stretch, Hearts and Bones, Urban Gothic, NCS Manhunt, Fun at the Funeral Parlour, The Last Detective, Doctors, New Tricks, The Bill, Hotel Babylon, Casualty, Katy Brand's Big Ass Show, 12 O'clock Girls, Green Santa, Little Crackers: My First Nativity, Coming Up (Hooked), Sadie J, Moving On, Pompidou, Holby City, Armada, Call The Midwife, The Worst Witch* and two series of *The Rebel*.

Film credits include: *Seaview Knights, Beyond Bedlam, The Tichborne Claimant, The Revengers' Comedies, Darkness Falls, Charlie, Solitary, The Rise of the Krays, The Fall of the Krays, London Road* taken from the acclaimed National Theatre production directed by Rufus Norris, and *The Fight*.

MAISIE RICHARDSON-SELLERS
Laurie

Maisie Richardson-Sellers studied Anthropology and Archaeology at Oxford University. Whilst there she was an avid member of the theatre community, both directing and performing, and appeared in a number of plays including *Mephisto* (Oxford Playhouse), *They Will Be Red* (Burton Taylor Studio) and *For Colored Girls Who Have Considered Suicide* (Oxford Union). Upon graduating she landed the role of Korr Sella in *Star Wars: The Force Awakens*. Since then she has been based in the United States and has performed the roles of Rebekah Mikaelson and Eva Sinclair in *The Originals* (The CW), Michal in *Of Kings and Prophets* (ABC) and Vixen/Amaya Jiwe in DC's *Legends of Tomorrow* (The CW). She is thrilled to be returning to the stage for *3Women*.

CREATIVES

KATY BRAND
Writer

Katy Brand is an award-winning writer, actor and comedian. She has appeared in numerous films, (*Nanny McPhee and the Big Bang*), TV shows (*Katy Brand's Big Ass Show*, *Peep Show*, *Grandpa's Great Escape*) and radio programmes (*News Quiz*, *The Infinite Monkey Cage*). Her critically acclaimed live work includes her 2016 show *I Was a Teenage Christian* ("*Intelligent storytelling.*" *The Times*). She has also written for many TV and radio shows, including her own. She is the author of *Brenda Monk is Funny*, her debut novel published in 2014 ("*Compulsive and absolutely essential.*" Irvine Welsh).

3Women is her first play.

MICHAEL YALE
Director

Michael Yale most recently directed the play *Late Company* at Trafalgar Studios (Broadway World Award nomination, shortlisted for Best New Production of a Play 2017).

Other work as director includes: *Late Company* (Finborough Theatre – OffWestEnd Award finalist), *This Little Life of Mine* (Park Theatre – multi-award nominations, including Best Director, Broadway World Awards and Best New Musical, Broadway World and OffWestEnd Awards), *Thrice Ninth Kingdom* (Soho Theatre and Tristan Bates Theatre), *Henry IV: Part One* (Rose Playhouse Bankside, and St. James Theatre), *Baby Mine* (Omnibus Theatre), *The Disappeared* (Theatre503), *Maternity* (Riverside Studios), *Wicked Will* (BAC and Tour),

Hell's Kitchen (Midlands Art Centre), and the award-winning *Monsieur D'Eon* (Union Theatre).

Michael is co-artistic director and founding member of Stage Traffic Productions. He trained at LAMDA and continues to act and write for theatre and television.

EILENE DAVIDSON
Producer and Creative Director

Eilene trained at drama school and worked as an actress, performing on stage and screen in her twenties. She then moved to the States and studied playwriting and screenwriting and worked as a freelance writer and playwright. Her company, Stage Traffic, was set up in 2016 to showcase new writing. Recently produced acclaimed plays include *This Little Life of Mine* (Park Theatre, London) and *Late Company* (Trafalgar Studios, London). Through her work with Stage Traffic, Eilene has a commitment to exclusively producing new writing from around the world. As an independent producer, Eilene has also produced or co-produced *A Lie of the Mind* (Southwark Playhouse), *Insignificance* (Langham, NYC), *WarPaint* (Nederland Theatre NYC), *Apologia* (Trafalgar Studios) and *The Grinning Man* currently showing in London (Trafalgar Studios). In 2018 Eilene is producing *Monogamy* (Park Theatre and tour), *Paper Dolls* (Mosaic Theatre, Washington DC) and this October she will produce the award-nominated European premiere of *A Guide for the Homesick* in a transfer from the USA to London.

STAGE TRAFFIC PRODUCTIONS

Stage Traffic Productions is a dynamic new UK/US theatre production company. Based in London, but looking at inspiration from around the globe, it is committed to creating productions with a strong emphasis on contemporary storytelling that truly resonates with modern audiences. The company's last production, *Late Company* (Trafalgar Studios), was met with universal critical acclaim and has made the shortlist for Best New Production of a Play at this year's Broadway World Awards. The company's inaugural production was the musical *This Little Life of Mine*, which ran at the Park Theatre in 2016. The show was nominated for many awards, including Best New Musical Production, OffWestEnd Awards and Best Musical, Best Director and Best Actress, Broadway World Awards. Eilene and Michael first met as actors eighteen years ago and since then both have worked additionally in the role of writer, director and producer, both in the States and the UK.

SUSANNA GULLIFORD
Marketing and PR Director

Susanna has over fifteen years' PR and marketing experience. She spent ten years at WPP as a director of Cohn & Wolfe, consulting for a number of major entertainment brands including the BBC, Sky, Orange, O2, Samsung, Northcliffe Media and the Rank Group. She moved to the Daily Mail General Trust in 2005 as Media Director, where she was responsible for launching and developing a number of new online brands. Susanna has worked with Stage Traffic Productions on *This Little Life of Mine* (2016) and *Late Company* (2017).

SARAH REED
Assistant Producer

Sarah has worked with Stage Traffic Productions on *Late Company* (Trafalgar Studios and Finborough Theatre) and *This Little Life of Mine* (Park Theatre). Stage management roles include *Absolution* and *Bill Clinton Hercules* (Park Theatre), *The Odd Couple* (CW Entertainment), *Austen's Women* (Leicester Square Theatre) and *One Flew Over the Cuckoo's Nest* (Really Useful Group). Her previous work with Theatre Tours International involved preparing their Edinburgh Festival season of shows, such as the Fringe First Award winner *Follow Me* (Assembly Rooms), while touring domestically and abroad. Sarah is very happy to be working again with Stage Traffic Productions at Trafalgar Studios.

ZAHRA MANSOURI
Set and Costume Designer

Trained at Central Saint Martins. Theatre includes the OffWestEnd Award-nominated *This Little Life of Mine* (Park Theatre), *The Cause* (Jermyn Street Theatre), *American Wife* (National and International Tour) and *The Marked* (Pleasance Edinburgh and Ovalhouse). Costume design for film includes *Shadowplan*, *The Movie Trilogy* and *Scrooge and the Seven Dwarves*. Zahra is also Associate Designer for Fourth Monkey Theatre Company, designing for their repertory seasons, and was also Assistant to the Designer for Trevor Nunn's *King John* (Rose Theatre, Kingston). www.zahramansouri.com.

NIC FARMAN
Lighting Designer

Nic is winner of The Worshipful Company of Lightmongers & ALD Award for New Talent in Entertainment Lighting 2016 and winner of the Francis Reid Award as part of the Association of Lighting Designers Michael Northen Bursary in 2013. Nic was also nominated for Best Lighting Designer at the OffWestEnd Awards in 2016 for *The Spanish Tragedy* and in 2015 for *Shock Treatment* and *The Win Bin*. Credits include: *The Toxic Avenger* (Arts Theatre and Southwark Playhouse); *Spring Awakening* (Hope Mill Theatre, Manchester); *Liver Birds Flying Home* (Liverpool Royal Court); *Tonight: The Eighties* (National Theatre, Jaber Al-Ahmad Cultural Centre, Kuwait); *Working* (Southwark Playhouse); *How to Succeed in Business without Really Trying* (Wilton's Music Hall); *Priscilla* (ArtsEd Andrew Lloyd Webber Foundation Theatre); *La Bohème* (Trafalgar Studios and King's Head Theatre); *Kindertransport* (Queen's Theatre, Hornchurch, Les Théâtres de la Ville de Luxembourg and UK Tour); *The Invisible Man* (Queen's Theatre, Hornchurch); *Late Company* (Trafalgar Studios and Finborough Theatre); *Shock Treatment*, Puccini's *Madame Butterfly, Così fan tutte* (King's Head Theatre); *Jack and the Beanstalk* (Salisbury Playhouse).

ELLIE COLLYER-BRISTOW CDG
Casting Director

Recent credits include: *Dusty* (UK Tour), *Monogamy* (Park Theatre and UK Tour), *Turn of the Screw* (Mercury Theatre and UK Tour), *Witness for the Prosecution* (County Hall, Southbank), children's casting for *The King and I* (London Palladium), *Jack and the Beanstalk* (Salisbury Playhouse), *Cookies* (Theatre Royal, Haymarket), *Wait Until Dark* (UK Tour), *Wordsworth, Two Way Mirror, After the Dance, As You Like It, Handbagged, Remarkable Invisible, Miss Julie* and *The Secret Garden* (Theatre by the Lake), *A Lie of the Mind* and *Doubt: A Parable* (Southwark Playhouse), *Madame Rubinstein* (Park Theatre), *Dirty Great Love Story* (Arts Theatre), *Fool for Love* (Found 111), children's casting for *The Wind in the Willows* (London Palladium), *Much Ado About Nothing* (ReFASHIONed Theatre @ Selfridges for The Faction), *French without Tears* (Orange Tree/ETT – UK Tour), *Night Must Fall* (Salisbury Playhouse/Original Theatre Company – UK Tour), *Sideways* (St James Theatre), *Gaslight* (Ed Mirvish, Toronto), *The Glass Menagerie* (Nuffield, Southampton), *Dancing at Lughnasa* (Lyric Theatre, Belfast), *Handbagged* (Eleanor Lloyd Productions – UK Tour), *The Gathered Leaves* (Park Theatre), *Arcadia* (ETT – UK Tour), *Told Look Younger* (Jermyn Street Theatre), *Eldorado* (Arcola Theatre), *Tape* (Trafalgar Studios), *Blue Remembered Hills, Playhouse Creatures* and *Fred's Diner* (Chichester Festival Theatre), *Four Nights in Knaresborough* (Southwark Playhouse); *Fings Ain't Wot They Used T'Be* and *Bernarda Alba* (Union Theatre); *This Is How It Goes* and *A Christmas Carol* (King's Head Theatre).

Ellie was previously Casting Associate for the Ambassador Theatre Group.

3WOMEN

A Play

by Katy Brand

||SAMUEL FRENCH||

samuelfrench.co.uk

THINKING ABOUT PERFORMING A SHOW?

There are thousands of plays and musicals available to perform from Samuel French right now, and applying for a licence is easier and more affordable than you might think

From classic plays to brand new musicals, from monologues to epic dramas, there are shows for everyone.

Plays and musicals are protected by copyright law so if you want to perform them, the first thing you'll need is a licence. This simple process helps support the playwright by ensuring they get paid for their work, and means that you'll have the documents you need to stage the show in public.

Not all our shows are available to perform all the time, so it's important to check and apply for a licence before you start rehearsals or commit to doing the show.

LEARN MORE & FIND THOUSANDS OF SHOWS

Browse our full range of plays and musicals and find out more about how to license a show

www.samuelfrench.co.uk/perform

Talk to the friendly experts in our Licensing team for advice on choosing a show, and help with licensing

plays@samuelfrench.co.uk   020 7387 9373

Acting Editions

BORN TO PERFORM

Playscripts designed from the ground up to work the way you do in rehearsal, performance and study

---

Larger, clearer text for easier reading

Wider margins for notes

Performance features such as character and props lists, sound and lighting cues, and more

---

+ CHOOSE A SIZE AND STYLE TO SUIT YOU

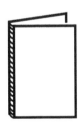

STANDARD EDITION

Our regular paperback book at our regular size

SPIRAL-BOUND EDITION

The same size as the Standard Edition, but with a sturdy, easy-to-fold, easy-to-hold spiral-bound spine

LARGE EDITION

A4 size and spiral bound, with larger text and a blank page for notes opposite every page of text. Perfect for technical and directing use

LEARN MORE | **samuelfrench.co.uk/actingeditions**

CHARACTERS

SUZANNE – forty, a bit soft and scruffy. Laurie's mother.
Eleanor's daughter.

ELEANOR – sixty-five, elegant and well put together.
Suzanne's mother. Laurie's grandmother.

LAURIE – eighteen, androgynous but delicate, ideally mixed-heritage. Suzanne's daughter. Eleanor's granddaughter.

RUFUS – twenty, a room service waiter who is striking and androgynous. A young man who is drifting but open.

ACKNOWLEDGEMENTS

Thanks to Eilene Davidson and Stage Traffic for commissioning and producing *3Women*, and supporting it all the way, along with Michael Yale for directing the first production and all the excellent script feed back. Thanks to the actors Anita Dobson, Debbie Chazen, Maisie Richardson-Sellers and Oliver Greenall for being the first to interpret the characters and performing them so brilliantly.

Thanks to Sarah Reed for wonderful Stage Management, Zahra Mansouri for beautiful design and Nic Farman for the sensitive lighting. Thanks to all at Emma Holland PR, Maidwell Marketing and Susanna Gulliford for letting people know about *3Women*. Thanks to Feast Creative for the artwork design. Thanks to Ellie Collyer-Bristow for all the help with casting the first production. Thanks to Trafalgar Studios for giving *3Women* its first home and being so fantastically supportive of new writing. Thanks to my agent Mandy Ward and all at Mandy Ward Artist Management. Thanks to Samuel French for publishing the play and being so enthusiastic.

Thanks to David, my husband and all important First Reader, and Skye and Thomas, for always being an inspiration. Finally thanks to all my female friends and family – I couldn't have done it without you.

For any woman in pursuit of her own happiness.

viii

Lights up.

It is early evening in a smart hotel suite – we are in the living room area, where there are a couple of sofas, a couple of armchairs, a coffee table. There are two large vases of flowers. There are three doors leading off from this area – one to the corridor, and two to the bedrooms.

The door to the corridor opens and a room service WAITER *enters with a bottle of champagne in a clear plastic ice bucket, three champagne flutes, and three roses, one white, one red and one yellow. He is a bit androgynous and quite striking, but smart in his uniform.*

He places the champagne flutes carefully on the coffee table with the ice bucket, and then consults a note on a small piece of paper. Following instructions, he delicately places one rose stem in each flute in this order: white, red, yellow. He places a small card on the table.

There is some light scratching and scraping on the outside of the door to the corridor. There is some muttered swearing outside too. The door handle on the corridor door starts being violently pushed up and down.

The room service WAITER *goes and opens the door.* SUZANNE *bursts in with her luggage, flustered and embarrassed, waving a credit-card-style key. She is carrying one too many bags, and her clothes are a bit all over the place. She wears a floaty, fringed scarf that has caught round her neck, throttling her slightly.*

SUZANNE Why don't these stupid keys ever work?

*She dumps her bags with a thud and fights to disentangle
herself from the never-ending scarf.*

WAITER   I think...

SUZANNE   *(startled)* Oh hello!

WAITER   I think...if you just tap it against the...

He gestures to the card and door as he speaks.

SUZANNE   I did, I did, I did tap it, I tapped it a thousand
times – I'm not smart enough for these types of places...
Are you supposed to be in my room?

WAITER   Sorry madame, I had to...

He trails off as he gestures to the arrangement of roses.
SUZANNE *finally gets free of the scarf and looks around
her, suddenly brought up short by how lovely the room is.*

SUZANNE   Goodness me.

The WAITER expertly gathers up SUZANNE's pile of bags.

WAITER   Will you take the single room, madame, or the double
room?

SUZANNE   The double, please, yes the double.

The WAITER nods and takes the bags to the double room.

SUZANNE *continues to look round the room. She notices
the roses and goes over to the table. She picks up the card,
reads it, and places it over her heart, touched.*

The WAITER re-enters.

WAITER   You have a nice view of the park...

SUZANNE *goes over to the window, and looks out at the
dusky light.*

SUZANNE   This must've cost him a fortune...

WAITER Your champagne is on the table, madame...

SUZANNE *turns to see it. She smiles, slightly bashfully. She seems to brush away a tear – she is moved by it all.*

SUZANNE It's lovely. It's just lovely.

WAITER If there is anything else I can get for you?

SUZANNE *(in a daze)* What? Oh, no – not at the moment, thank you.

WAITER Would you like me to open your champagne for you?

SUZANNE *(slightly giddy, playful)* No, thanks – Oh! Unless you can do that thing where you slice off the end of the bottle with a sword?

She mimes doing this, as she has seen on TV. It is quite a strong motion outwards, and the WAITER *flinches a bit.*

WAITER *(baffled)* Uh, no, I don't think... We don't keep any swords in the hotel...

SUZANNE That's probably just as well.

WAITER *(slightly nervous)* Yes. Shall I...?

He indicates the champagne.

SUZANNE No, no – I'll do it. Don't worry, thank you.

He turns to go. He reaches the door when SUZANNE *comes to her senses.*

Wait, sorry – here, let me give you...

She grabs her purse and rummages in it.

God, I never carry cash anymore – hang on, sorry.

She rummages a bit more and finds a couple of pound coins. She counts out another pound in silvers. He waits patiently.

Is that alright? Sorry.

WAITER Thank you very much, madame. Please just call down
  if you would like anything else.

SUZANNE Thank you.

*He leaves. She looks around again, touching the beautiful
sofas, and smelling the vases of flowers. She looks at the
three champagne flutes, taking in the roses. She picks the
bottle up from its ice bucket. She hesitates for a minute
before removing the red rose from its flute. Then she stops
herself, puts the bottle back in the bucket unopened and
places the red rose back in the flute, exactly as it was.*

She calls room service.

Hello, yes it's Suzanne Lloyd in the Taylor Suite – could I
have a large gin and tonic please? Thank you.

She hangs up.

The door opens and in walks ELEANOR, *elegant and
unhurried, in a beautifully cut pair of trousers, silk
blouse, immaculate hair and make-up. She is followed by
the same* WAITER, *who is carrying her perfectly formed
overnight bag.*

SUZANNE *is slightly taken aback.*

Mother! How did you...?

The WAITER *hurriedly takes her bag into the other
(single) room in the suite.*

ELEANOR God, they gave me murder downstairs about giving
  me a key – I honestly think hotels are trying to keep people
  out these days.

  I said, "It may be in *her name* but she is *my daughter*, and
  I need to speak to her urgently."

As she speaks, ELEANOR *has got out her purse, removed
a couple of coins, and is now holding them out as the*
WAITER *returns and passes her. She smoothly drops*

*them into his hand, he nods, and exits. This is all a bit
of a blur.* SUZANNE *can't quite keep up.*

SUZANNE But...but how did the key work?

ELEANOR What?

SUZANNE On the door?

ELEANOR Oh, you just tap it, darling.

SUZANNE *nods – of course.*

SUZANNE So what did you want to speak to me about so
urgently?

ELEANOR You've lost me.

SUZANNE You said you told the receptionist that you had to
speak me urgently.

ELEANOR *considers this for a moment – she had forgotten.
Then the penny drops.*

ELEANOR Ah yes, so I did! Oh nothing, darling – don't panic. It's
just something I say – I find things happen more efficiently
if I look like I might make a scene.

SUZANNE I can imagine.

ELEANOR *is oblivious, or seems to be.*

So, there's nothing then?

ELEANOR Nothing. Nothing that can't wait.

SUZANNE *nods, slightly suspicious.* ELEANOR *presses on.*

Well, let me look at you, on this auspicious evening.

She looks SUZANNE *up and down.*

Ok, ok – have you got some good underwear for tomorrow?
Because it makes all the difference...

There's a soft knock at the door. SUZANNE *opens it,
takes the gin and tonic straight off the tray at the door,*

scribbles a signature and shuts the door again. She takes a large sip.

ELEANOR *is looking at the roses in flutes.*

Are these from...

SUZANNE Gary, yes, there's a note...

She looks around – it's here somewhere. ELEANOR *doesn't need the note.*

ELEANOR Very clever.

SUZANNE What is?

ELEANOR The red for you, of course, the virginal white for Laurie, and the funereal yellow for me...

SUZANNE I don't think he meant it like that...

ELEANOR Did you know in Russia it's considered extremely bad luck to send yellow roses? Totally taboo. It almost amounts to a threat...

SUZANNE *(faintly)* No, I didn't know that. I don't think Gary wants you dead.

ELEANOR Give him time – he barely knows me.

SUZANNE *drinks from her gin and tonic again.*

SUZANNE Have you seen the view?

ELEANOR *goes to the window.*

ELEANOR The park. Yes lovely. They used to have such beautiful lights there years ago, strung along between the trees. Can't see much in the dark now...

SUZANNE Probably an environmental thing. Or council cuts – something like that.

ELEANOR It's a shame, anyway.

ELEANOR *turns back to* SUZANNE. *An awkward moment of silence – neither quite knows what to say to the other. Conversation does not come easily or naturally.*

A knock at the door – saved!

SUZANNE Ah! – this'll be her. Here she is.

SUZANNE *goes to open it with nervous energy.* LAURIE *walks in, full of natural confidence, perhaps even a slight hint of teenage swagger, a bit of bounce to her. She has an androgynous quality – no make-up, very short hair, wears a very plain dress or trousers, an oversized lumberjack shirt, with thick socks and heavy boots. She dumps a duffel bag on the floor.* SUZANNE *throws her arms around her.* LAURIE *hugs back, tightly.*

LAURIE Mum – or should I say, blushing bride?

SUZANNE Hello, my baby – just in time...

SUZANNE *engulfs* LAURIE *again in a huge, all-encompassing hug, kissing her on the cheek, from which* LAURIE *has to good-naturedly struggle free.*

LAURIE For what? It's not til tomorrow morning...right?

SUZANNE Yes, yes, that's right, tomorrow morning, yes, ah it's good to see you – I've missed you. I've missed you.

LAURIE *(laughing)* It's only been a few weeks, Mum... Hi, Grandma.

ELEANOR, *by contrast with* SUZANNE, *allows* LAURIE *to approach her, and turns her cheek slightly to allow* LAURIE *to kiss it – no body contact at all.*

ELEANOR Hello darling, let me look at you.

She stands back and looks LAURIE *up and down, just as she did with* SUZANNE.

Very modern.

She smiles and **LAURIE** *smiles back, taking it as a compliment, which it sort of is, or as close to compliments as* **ELEANOR** *will get.*

SUZANNE Right, we're all here now, so let's open the fizz!

She drains her glass of gin and tonic and pulls the bottle from its bucket.

LAURIE *picks up the red rose by the stem.*

Careful – thorns.

LAURIE *looks – no thorns.*

ELEANOR They cut the thorns off roses at the smart places – makes them easier to handle.

LAURIE *looks closer.*

LAURIE Oh yeah – nice. Nice touch.

She puts her nose in the rose to smell it.

ELEANOR That one's your mother's. They're from Gary.

LAURIE *drops it like it's hot, suddenly embarrassed that she assumed it was for her.*

LAURIE Oh! Sorry.

ELEANOR The white one's yours... It's meant to be virginal.

LAURIE *smirks knowingly.*

LAURIE That's...nice. What's the yellow one mean, then?

ELEANOR *goes to speak.* **SUZANNE** *cuts her off.*

SUZANNE Nevermind that...

She pulls the three roses from their flutes with one hand and drops them lightly on the coffee table. She pours three glasses of champagne, and they each take one.

SUZANNE To...to...to...

ELEANOR *(drily)* Wedded bliss?

SUZANNE ...second chances...

ELEANOR I'll drink to that.

They raise their glasses and drink.

LAURIE So, where is Gary tonight anyway? Last night of freedom – Vegas? Dubai?

SUZANNE Hitchin.

LAURIE Hitchin.

SUZANNE *laughs.*

SUZANNE Gary's not really a very Vegas kind of guy.

ELEANOR Glad to hear it...

SUZANNE He wanted to just be at home, with his brothers and a couple of mates.

LAURIE Wild. So he got this for us?

She looks around.

Sweet.

SUZANNE He wanted us to have a night together, you know, just the three of us. Family time.

ELEANOR *and* LAURIE *nod, but don't quite connect with the idea somehow.*

LAURIE Cool – so is Uncle John not coming too then?

SUZANNE No, no – it's for us women. A bit of female bonding.

LAURIE Is he coming tomorrow? I haven't seen him for ages.

SUZANNE Yes, I think so – he said he was.

ELEANOR Ah lovely – what a treat to see him.

SUZANNE Don't get your hopes up, Mother – he'll slide in ten minutes before it starts, charm the pants off everyone, and then slide off ten minutes before the end, like he always does.

LAURIE He cracks me up, though.

SUZANNE Me too, darling – I wasn't trying to be...

ELEANOR Your brother's a very busy man, Suzanne. He works hard. And he's in the middle of a house sale right now – he can't just drop everything at a moment's notice.

SUZANNE *rolls her eyes.*

SUZANNE Yes, well, anyway – family's a big deal for Gary – it's important to him. He likes having a tribe. Maybe it's sensible – like an old survival technique. He thinks I should make more...

LAURIE *(cutting her off with enthusiasm)* I once read that we are all descended from either hiders or fighters, because everyone else just gets killed or captured.

SUZANNE That's funny – I wonder which ones we are?

ELEANOR Hiders.

LAURIE Fighters.

They say this simultaneously and they all laugh a little.

ELEANOR Is he from a big family – Gary?

SUZANNE Three brothers and a sister.

ELEANOR Goodness – are his parents Catholic?

SUZANNE No, just wanted lots of kids.

ELEANOR *looks mystified, bordering on appalled. She almost shudders.*

ELEANOR I suppose it's easier in a big family.

LAURIE What's easier?

ELEANOR Well, to...to...get along, I suppose. More people, more things to talk about.

Another slightly awkward pause. SUZANNE *and* LAURIE *exchange a wry, amused glance. They all drink.* LAURIE *changes the energy, grabbing her mother's hand impulsively and squeezing it.*

LAURIE So, are you nervous?

SUZANNE A bit. It's a big thing, getting married. I think that's only just fully dawned on me.

ELEANOR The biggest... Well, that and buying a house.

SUZANNE I wouldn't know...

ELEANOR No...

SUZANNE I can't see me ever buying a house.

ELEANOR No...

SUZANNE I guess older people bought them cheap and are going to just cling onto them for life.

ELEANOR By older people, I assume you mean me and your father?

SUZANNE How are those four bedrooms, Mum?

ELEANOR Well, one of them's yours.

SUZANNE But I don't live there now.

ELEANOR We've all had hard times, you know – the 70s, my god – I won't even bore you with it...

SUZANNE *goes quiet.*

LAURIE I don't think I'll ever bother buying a house – I can just live somewhere exciting where the rents are cheaper.

ELEANOR Such as?

LAURIE Barcelona. Estonia. Anywhere really – I don't want to be chained to a desk my whole life, just to die in a suburban box with my name on it.

ELEANOR How will you work?

LAURIE I'll do it all from my laptop. Or even my watch.

> LAURIE *holds out her wrist with a smartwatch on it.*
> ELEANOR *shakes her head.*

ELEANOR I'll look forward to you filing your annual accounts from a zip wire in Cambodia.

LAURIE So will I.

ELEANOR Well, anyway, I'm selling the house now, so if you want to buy it, Suzanne, you're more than welcome.

SUZANNE Selling the house? Since when?

ELEANOR Like you say – I don't need all that space to myself. It's not as if you ever come and visit, is it?

> SUZANNE *looks away, guilty.*

And anyway I want a warmer climate.

SUZANNE What are you talking about?

ELEANOR Yes, I have an announcement of my own to make actually: I'm moving to Italy.

LAURIE Wow.

SUZANNE What?

ELEANOR I wasn't going to mention it tonight because, well, you know, it's supposed to be *your* special night etc, but now I've been cornered I might as well tell you – I'm selling the house and moving to Italy.

I've always wanted to retire to Italy and so now I've finished teaching, and your father's gone, what's stopping me? I can't stand another winter here.

> SUZANNE *and* LAURIE *take in this news.*

And in any case, Suzanne, you'll be moving in with Gary now, won't you? After the wedding tomorrow?

SUZANNE I mean, I'm there most of the time anyway. But officially, yes.

ELEANOR Well there you are then – what are you complaining about? You'll basically own a home through your husband. That's how most women in history have done it. And it's not as if you've been pursuing a lucrative career your whole life. I don't see how anyone could buy a house on dog walking, blogging and tie-dying T-shirts to sell on the internet. Not even in the "fabled 70s".

LAURIE Top-up?

ELEANOR *and* SUZANNE Yes please.

They hold up their glasses and LAURIE *fills them.*

SUZANNE Where in Italy?

ELEANOR Puglia.

SUZANNE Where's Puglia?

ELEANOR South – down in the heel of the boot, right in the spike. Beautiful food, sparkling sea, olive groves.

I went there once many years ago, before I met your father, and always vowed I'd go back.

SUZANNE Why didn't you go with him then?

ELEANOR Your father was such a terrible traveller – you remember. We couldn't fly, couldn't get on a boat, didn't much like driving, it was all I could do to get him on a train and even then we'd have to sit at the front.

SUZANNE Is that why we never went abroad?

ELEANOR That's why we never went anywhere.

SUZANNE Sorry, and now forty-five years later you're just going to turn up there and move in?

ELEANOR Not quite – I've made a few trips over the past couple of years, got to know...the place again.

SUZANNE *is completely blindsided.*

LAURIE Well, I think it's great, Grandma. Do something different before you die.

ELEANOR *(wry)* Thank you, darling. Yes, I must say I am excited to be beginning a new life. Well, in a way we all are. You at university, and your mother getting married and moving to...to...

SUZANNE Hitchin.

ELEANOR Hitchin.

A pause.

SUZANNE Well it's nice that you have a house to sell, so you can go off and do what you want.

ELEANOR You're starting to sound a little bitter, dear.

SUZANNE Am I? Shall we order another bottle, then?

ELEANOR Yes, that's a good idea. It's not the expensive stuff, is it? Might as well get two.

SUZANNE *notes the slight, and calls room service.*

SUZANNE Two bottles of the house Prosecco for the Taylor Suite, please, thank you, oh and the tapas selection, and the mini-pizzas, and the cheese board, thank you.

ELEANOR Don't get bloated the night before. You won't like the pictures...

SUZANNE We need to eat. People need to eat, Mother, or hadn't you heard?

ELEANOR *smooths down her neat figure and regards her daughter's somewhat softer physique.*

LAURIE I'm starving.

ELEANOR Well you got my genes dear, you're lucky like me – a fast metaboliser. It often skips a generation. It's harder as I get older, of course, but it's about discipline.

SUZANNE Uh-huh.

ELEANOR I'll have to watch it in Italy. Luckily Puglia is famous for its fish rather than its pasta. Gosh, I can't wait to have a glass of wine in the evening sun.

SUZANNE Does John know about this?

ELEANOR I might have mentioned it in an email. He's fully on board.

SUZANNE Oh right, so you told John.

ELEANOR Your brother responds to his emails from time to time. I didn't think you'd be interested, to be honest.

SUZANNE When are you going? I can't believe this.

ELEANOR Soon as I can. Don't make a fuss, Suzanne, not tonight. It's a family gathering – let's not argue, and waste Gary's generous gift.

Subject closed. SUZANNE *opens her mouth and closes it again. Instead she pours herself another drink.* ELEANOR *sips her wine and turns to* LAURIE.

Come and sit next to your Grandma and tell me all about your life. What about university? How's it going?

She pats the space next to her on the sofa. LAURIE *sits down.*

LAURIE Oh my god, I love it – I mean it's only been a month, but I love it.

ELEANOR Are you in halls?

LAURIE Private student flats – they build them new, just for students.

ELEANOR When I went to university, we had to live in halls or nothing, and it was girls only. I shared a room with a girl I'd never met before the first day! Can you imagine?

SUZANNE Who was that?

ELEANOR Lorraine, she was called.

SUZANNE I don't remember you mentioning her – did you keep in touch?

ELEANOR Not really – I met your father and that was that. She wanted more of a career, but I'd got married and had you before I really knew what I was doing. She's something high up in the Civil Service now. My grades were better than hers, but in those days you couldn't do both. Not like now.

SUZANNE Still can't.

ELEANOR Some can...

That was a jab at SUZANNE.

LAURIE Well, these student flats are cool – you get your own room and bathroom, and share a kitchen, and there's a gym downstairs for us to use.

ELEANOR You really have got it all sorted!

SUZANNE It's bloody expensive.

ELEANOR It sounds it.

SUZANNE She's worth every penny, though.

ELEANOR You were very expensive at university, too. Your father had to work extra hours, and I saved whatever I could.

SUZANNE Once the wine had been bought, of course.

ELEANOR *looks up sharply. There's a knock. Room service is here.* LAURIE *opens the door.*

ELEANOR Isn't there some sort of student grant you can get though? If the parent is unemployed?

SUZANNE I'm not unemployed.

ELEANOR Well you know what I mean. If you don't have a proper job.

SUZANNE I'm freelance.

ELEANOR Yes, darling, but freelance what?

SUZANNE I don't know – anything that will pay. It's best to stay flexible in this world. To be adaptable.

ELEANOR Really? And there's me thinking it's best to pick something and stick to it – to really master it. But perhaps I'm old-fashioned.

The room service WAITER *is in the room (same one as at the beginning), pushing a trolley with food and drink on it.*

LAURIE Mum, can you sign for this?

SUZANNE Oh yes, sorry.

She mentally calculates a tip and then scribbles her name.

LAURIE *walks to the door with him.*

LAURIE Thanks.

WAITER No problem.

A moment between them of mutual attraction. ELEANOR *has observed this. He goes.*

ELEANOR He gave you the eye, there. At least, I think it was a "he". Never too sure these days.

SUZANNE It's called gender fluidity, Mother. Keep up.

ELEANOR Is that what you are?

She is addressing LAURIE, *but not unpleasantly.*

LAURIE Yeah. I don't like to define myself by heteronormative traditions.

ELEANOR I see. Well I have no idea what that means.

LAURIE It basically says that male and female are the accepted norm, and I don't go along with that. "If you can't describe it, you can't fight it" – that's what we say.

SUZANNE Who's this?

LAURIE Just a bunch of people from uni – like a sort of protest group.

SUZANNE *(genuinely interested)* Oh right – what do you protest against?

LAURIE Anything that needs changing. But at the moment we want gender-neutral toilets in all university buildings.

ELEANOR I'm not sure I'd like that – a bit of mystery doesn't do any harm between men and women.

LAURIE But we don't want mystery – we want to be open and free. It's not about men and women anymore – just people.

ELEANOR But if you and that waiter got together, I wouldn't know what I was looking at. I wouldn't know what went where in the bedroom.

LAURIE Grandma!

She is laughing a little bit. ELEANOR *is opening a bottle and picking at the food.*

ELEANOR You've got such a beautiful face, Laurie, I don't know why you don't want to look like a woman.

LAURIE *(teasing)* Do you mean I should have long hair? And wear flowery dresses?

ELEANOR Well, not exactly. But don't men find this whole look at a bit...off-putting?

LAURIE I've never had any trouble so far...

ELEANOR So far? You're eighteen! How much "so far" can there be?

LAURIE Well, I like sex – just because I dress like this, doesn't mean I don't want...y'know, "experiences" with other people. I want to connect, any way I can, whenever I get the chance. It's good for you.

ELEANOR Aren't you worried people will think you're a bit of a...well, a bit of a *(hesitates)* "slut"?

LAURIE Liking sex doesn't make a person a slut, Grandma – we should all just do it whenever we feel like it, however we want to. I think it would solve a lot of problems, actually. Regular orgasms for everyone would definitely lead to world peace and harmony.

She is sort of joking, but ELEANOR *is serious.*

ELEANOR Perhaps, but the men may not agree so readily. Not the marrying kind anyway.

SUZANNE Mother, you sound so old-fashioned.

ELEANOR You're not helping her by trying to be all hip and cool and pretending otherwise. A husband can come in useful in life, you know.

SUZANNE I know, that's why I'm getting myself one tomorrow morning.

ELEANOR *nods.*

ELEANOR I'd almost given up hope.

SUZANNE *shrugs.*

LAURIE I don't really expect to be with one person for my whole life.

ELEANOR But don't you want the companionship? The security?

LAURIE I'm alright – I've got friends. And I've got companionship whenever I want it right here, on this.

She holds up her phone.

ELEANOR So you just pick and choose who you want, when you want? You don't rely on anyone?

LAURIE Too much pressure – I just swipe right and move on – I don't want to disappoint anyone, and I don't want to be disappointed.

ELEANOR There speaks a fatherless child.

SUZANNE I didn't want to be disappointed either.

ELEANOR Well, that's your own doing. You've always had a taste for unreliable men.

LAURIE Who says my father was unreliable?

ELEANOR Well he didn't exactly stick around to face up to his responsibilities, did he?

SUZANNE I'm not surprised after the dressing down he got from Dad.

ELEANOR His little girl was pregnant.

SUZANNE Not little – I was twenty-two.

ELEANOR Twenty-two is a baby.

SUZANNE You were twenty-five.

ELEANOR I was married. We had our own house. Your father had a good job. That's different.

SUZANNE I don't think I've done a bad job. Just look at her.

ELEANOR *and* SUZANNE *look at* LAURIE *just as she is stuffing a handful of salsa-drenched nachos into her mouth. She laughs as the tomato sauce drips down her chin at how she has spoiled this moment. They all laugh.*

ELEANOR No, you're right – she's something to be proud of. For us all to be proud of. I'm proud of you, darling.

This is directed at LAURIE, *and also has the effect of excluding* SUZANNE. SUZANNE *sighs and her shoulders drop.*

LAURIE You did an alright job, Mum, I'll give you that.

ELEANOR Motherhood is hard for everyone. I know I was grateful to my mother too, and I told her so.

She waits for some good word from **SUZANNE**. *It is not forthcoming.*

Yes, well, shall we have a look at this awful spread, then? A symphony of complex carbohydrates.

ELEANOR *looks at the food. She prods a couple of bits, and then takes a piece of Parma ham, wraps it up and eats it.*

Not as good as the real Italian stuff, of course.

SUZANNE Of course.

SUZANNE *picks up a piece of cheese-laden pizza and thrusts it at her mother.* **ELEANOR** *shakes her head.* **SUZANNE** *pushes it further.*

You sure? It smells wonderful.

ELEANOR *jumps back as if it's a dangerous snake, with her hands up.*

ELEANOR Don't come at me, Suzanne, don't come at me with food.

SUZANNE *(laughing at her)* It's not a weapon, Mum. It's a slice of pizza.

SUZANNE *bites into it herself.*

ELEANOR Yes, alright, you've made your point.

She edges round the room so that there is furniture between herself and **SUZANNE**, *and delicately picks up an olive.*

LAURIE Mum, what are you wearing tomorrow, then?

SUZANNE Do you want to see?

LAURIE Do you even have to ask?

SUZANNE *goes through one of the doors that leads to a bedroom.*

ELEANOR What are *you* wearing?

LAURIE I got a lovely suit from the British Heart Foundation.

ELEANOR A charity shop? Don't they smell funny? I always assume someone's died in it.

LAURIE I had it dry-cleaned. It's still good value, even after that.

ELEANOR *shudders a bit.*

ELEANOR A...suit...for a woman, or...?

LAURIE It's a man's suit, but I cropped the arms and legs and it's quite slim fitting, so it doesn't look like a – anyway, does it matter?

ELEANOR I'm sure you're right. But girls your age look good in anything. The rest of us, however...

She trails off as SUZANNE *returns with a clothes bag. She unzips it and pulls out a floaty, slightly hippyish dress in different shades of green and turquoise.*

SUZANNE Ta-daa! I didn't think white was appropriate.

ELEANOR No.

SUZANNE So? What do we think?

LAURIE It's gorgeous, Mum.

ELEANOR It's very...you.

LAURIE Did you get it from Astra?

SUZANNE Yes, they let me pay in instalments – so sweet. Well they know me.

ELEANOR What is "Astra"?

SUZANNE A shop near us – sells a mix of things, spiritual stuff, you know, crystals.

ELEANOR Pewter wizards, homeopathy oils and wotnot?

SUZANNE Yes, sort of.

ELEANOR Is that where you get all your knickknacks?

SUZANNE I wouldn't call them knickknacks – they keep me centred – some people use crystals, other people use wine.

Another sharp look from **ELEANOR.**

LAURIE It's going to look amazing.

ELEANOR You have to be very tall and slim to really carry off a big floaty number like that. Otherwise you look a bit like an impending tidal wave – you can frighten people. Have you got good underwear?

SUZANNE I want to be comfortable.

ELEANOR Comfortable?? On your wedding day?

SUZANNE Yes. And it's important to Gary, too. He will wear what he feels comfortable in as well – you'll see.

ELEANOR I can't wait.

SUZANNE makes an effort to be patient.

SUZANNE Mum, do you have a problem with all of this?

ELEANOR What makes to you say that, dear?

SUZANNE I feel that you have been very negative since you arrived, and you keep making these little remarks.

ELEANOR I don't know what you mean.

SUZANNE You know exactly what I mean.

LAURIE Mum...

SUZANNE No, sweetie, I have promised myself that as a married woman I am not going to just take things anymore.

ELEANOR You're being a bit dramatic, darling.

SUZANNE No, I'm not! Don't deny my point of view...

She has raised her voice.

ELEANOR Keep your voice down. You'll burst a blood vessel in your face and then you really won't like the pictures tomorrow.

SUZANNE I will *love* the pictures tomorrow, I will *love* them because they will be of me and Gary on our wedding day, and so I will be happy.

ELEANOR Alright, alright – sorry I spoke. Come on darling, let's not fight tonight. Let's have a top-up, come on.

> ELEANOR *gets the bottle and tops them all up. She raises her glass.*

To love, life and happiness! And being comfortable.

They all raise their glasses and drink.

LAURIE I've been kind of seeing someone, actually.

SUZANNE Oh yes?! Who?

LAURIE James.

ELEANOR James? James seems like a very conventional name for you – I'd've thought you go after someone called Nectarine, or Space Pixie or something like that.

LAURIE No, he's called James. But he was born Jane.

ELEANOR Ah yes, there it is.

LAURIE He's transitioning.

ELEANOR Of course.

SUZANNE *(warning)* Mother.

> ELEANOR *holds up her hands.*

So, how long have you been seeing James? I don't remember meeting anyone called James from school. Or Jane.

LAURIE We haven't met yet. He lives in Montreal. We've been virtually dating for about a month.

ELEANOR Oh I've bloody heard it all now.

LAURIE We Skype every day, and we did this VR thing the other night – it was wild. Like actually being in the same room.

ELEANOR You know, I was actually in the same room as your grandfather for most of our marriage, if you can imagine such an outmoded concept.

SUZANNE But you spent much of the time wishing you were in a different room, as far as I remember, so you're not really selling it.

ELEANOR Fair enough.

She's slightly drunk now. She refills her glass.

LAURIE He's coming over at some point, when he can afford it.

SUZANNE Are you sure you want to start university attached to someone, though?

ELEANOR Attached?! He's four thousand miles away!

LAURIE It's an open relationship.

ELEANOR I should think it is.

SUZANNE Well I would love to meet him when he comes.

ELEANOR *(sarcastic)* Let's all meet him together – we can all form a first impression of Laurie's "boyfriend" at the same time.

SUZANNE You're getting drunk.

ELEANOR I am not. It's just this cheap fizz has so much sugar in it, it gets into your bloodstream faster.

SUZANNE Oh *I've* heard it all now.

LAURIE Stop bitching, the pair of you. The whole point of this evening is to come together and celebrate Mum's big day like a family, like a proper family.

This brings them up short.

SUZANNE Sorry, darling.

ELEANOR Sorry.

A pause. Then back on it.

I just don't know what you see in him.

SUZANNE Here we go.

ELEANOR I only want what's best for you darling, and I wonder if you're settling.

SUZANNE Of course I'm settling – I'm forty.

ELEANOR When I met your father, I felt like I was made of meringue. All soft and sweet – he had that effect on me, when we first met. I just wish you'd had that experience.

SUZANNE I have had that experience, just not with Gary.

LAURIE Are you sure you should be marrying him then?

SUZANNE Yes – I love him. I just love him like a forty-year-old, not a twenty-two-year-old.

LAURIE But that was how old you were when you had me.

SUZANNE Yes.

LAURIE So, you felt like a meringue with my dad?

SUZANNE *hesitates.*

SUZANNE Yes. But then I got pregnant – which, darling, I wouldn't change for the world. But then it all came to an end – it happens. He wasn't a bad man.

ELEANOR Just irresponsible.

SUZANNE Not even that. He just wasn't ready for a baby.

ELEANOR Neither were you, but you had no choice.

LAURIE *waves her arms in the air, as if signalling for help.*

LAURIE Guys, *hello*! I'm right here – you're talking about *me*, you know.

SUZANNE And we love you.

ELEANOR Yes, we do. We all do. But why do we always say, "Suzanne got pregnant", as if she brushed against some mythical fertility fawn in a forest? Where's the man in that statement? Why not say, "Christian got Suzanne pregnant". Name him – name him so he can't disappear.

SUZANNE He didn't disappear – I knew where he went.

ELEANOR Where?

SUZANNE *and* LAURIE Berlin.

> SUZANNE *looks at* LAURIE, *surprised.*

LAURIE That's what you told me.

SUZANNE Did I? I don't remember telling you.

LAURIE *(covering)* You were a bit high at the time.

SUZANNE Oh.

> *She nods as if that explains it.*

ELEANOR Well, he never sent you any money.

SUZANNE He didn't have any money.

ELEANOR Then he should've kept it in his pants.

SUZANNE I wasn't on the pill.

ELEANOR Then you should have kept it in *your* pants.

LAURIE Guys – still me we're talking about here.

ELEANOR It was just such a waste, Suzanne. You were a bright girl, and we gave up so much to give you the best start in life, and then just out of university with your whole life ahead of you, you went and did that. My god – it has defined your whole life – one mistake, and it's all gone.

LAURIE Jesus, thanks.

> *She pours herself some more wine and drinks it all down.*

SUZANNE My daughter is not a mistake – look at her – she's a wonder. I brought life into this world – that is my achievement.

ELEANOR Any woman who can spread her legs and bear a little pain can bring life into the world, Suzanne, but how many are educated? How many have spark and drive? All those women of my generation denied a top-flight career, and you have everything in your lap and you just chuck it away.

SUZANNE Ok, here we go.

ELEANOR Here we go? Here we go? Yes indeed, here we go – I was the first woman in my family to go to university, the first – can you imagine?

SUZANNE Funnily enough, I can, because you might have mentioned it once or twice before...

ELEANOR *(not listening)* I bucked the trend of generations, and everyone said I was destined for something special, and I studied hard, I didn't waste a minute, I didn't drink a drop, I smoked nothing, I kept myself nice and I worked, I qualified. And then I met your father.

SUZANNE And you became a meringue.

ELEANOR Exactly, a meringue – soft and sweet, but also weak and liable to collapse, and I did collapse into his arms, like a stupid girl, and then along came you and your brother, and that was it.

SUZANNE I thought you liked teaching.

ELEANOR Oh, teaching was the only thing open to me by the time you two were at school. And even then I had to be home to get your father's tea – he was old-fashioned like that. But I was a good teacher, yes, I was, and I could've gone a lot further with it if...

SUZANNE ...you hadn't been drunk all the time.

An icy silence. This is new.

ELEANOR What did you say?

LAURIE Mum...?

SUZANNE I might as well say it then – I know why you didn't get promoted.

ELEANOR pales slightly, but maintains her composure.

ELEANOR Excuse me?

SUZANNE You always like to act as if you're some feminist martyr born at the wrong time, but the reason you didn't get promoted beyond subject teacher at the school is because they caught you teaching when you were drunk. Shit-faced in the classroom – reeking of booze and trying to tell a bunch of twelve-year-olds about the Norman Invasion.

ELEANOR is deadly still and quiet.

So don't blame me, is what I'm saying, or John or Dad. It's not our fault you never made good on your potential. It's because you were pissed all the time. At work, and at home. There, I said it. I said it.

She drinks.

ELEANOR *(lightly)* How did you know all that?

SUZANNE I found a letter tucked into a book at home once when I was looking for something. It was from the school – about the disciplinary hearing.

ELEANOR is nodding, making a show of listening.

ELEANOR When was this?

SUZANNE About ten years ago.

ELEANOR And you never said anything.

SUZANNE I didn't see the point.

ELEANOR *(brazening it out, a practised response)* It was a huge overreaction at the school. I'd just had a shot of vodka to take the edge off some toothache. Your father knew it was all a load of nonsense. You shouldn't read too much into it.

SUZANNE Toothache.

ELEANOR Toothache.

SUZANNE So you didn't used to drink during the day, in the morning, before the school run?

ELEANOR No.

SUZANNE So I am remembering that wrongly, then, am I?

ELEANOR You are very imaginative. It's one of your best qualities.

A hint of sarcasm there.

SUZANNE I see.

A pause. **LAURIE** *eyes them both carefully.*

ELEANOR I think...

SUZANNE Yes?

ELEANOR I think I need...

SUZANNE Mum, it's ok, let's leave it...

ELEANOR I think...I need a drink... A gin and tonic.

> **SUZANNE** *takes this in – it's not an apology – then nods mutely and picks up the phone to order her mother a gin and tonic.*

SUZANNE Ok.

ELEANOR A large one.

SUZANNE *(defeated)* Of course.

> **LAURIE** *looks from one to the other – what to do?*

LAURIE Shall we have some music?

ELEANOR Music, yes, good idea. Your dress is lovely, dear, and I'm sure you will feel very comfortable in it. Very comfortable indeed.

LAURIE *notices an iPod dock, and starts scrolling through her phone to find some music.*

LAURIE What do you like dancing to, Grandma? You'll have a dance?

ELEANOR No thanks, darling. I'll just go and freshen up a bit. A bit of lipstick can make all the difference.

SUZANNE Lipstick, is it? Ok.

ELEANOR *takes her handbag into her bedroom, shutting the door behind her.*

SUZANNE *moves closer to* LAURIE. *They talk intimately and naturally, like old mates.*

Hundred quid says she's got a little bottle of vodka in her handbag in there.

LAURIE You haven't got a hundred quid.

SUZANNE True.

LAURIE Is all that for real? Has she got a problem? I've never noticed.

SUZANNE Your grandmother redefines "high-functioning". She's in denial. Always has been.

LAURIE Shouldn't we get her some help?

SUZANNE She's beyond help.

LAURIE No one's beyond help.

SUZANNE She'll never admit she's got a problem. Self-analysis? She'd rather die of leprosy. I promised myself I'd never be like that.

LAURIE *finds a track she likes.*

LAURIE Ah this is a good one...

"HEART OF GLASS" by Blondie plays over the speaker. LAURIE *and* SUZANNE *dance together.*

Mum, do you really love Gary?

SUZANNE Of course. He's a good man. He's helped me a lot.

LAURIE But that doesn't mean you love him. Like with your whole being.

SUZANNE Oh sweetie, I know that's the dream. But as you get older you have to deal with reality.

LAURIE You can deal with reality without getting married to it.

SUZANNE I do. I will.

She throws her hands up. It is a positive moment that takes over and makes **SUZANNE** *and* **LAURIE** *dance again.*

Pause: The lights dim, as the music becomes an a cappella version of ***"HEART OF GLASS"*** *– just the vocals singing the chorus, with a little reverb. The actors move slowly but deliberately into new positions.* **ELEANOR** *also returns to the stage.*

Lights up.

We find the three women sat together, looking at a handful of old photographs, drinks in hand. **SUZANNE** *is examining a particular photo.*

Is that me or John?

ELEANOR That's you. Two hours old. I look an absolute wreck, don't I?

SUZANNE Not at all. Give yourself a break.

ELEANOR Gosh, I was ill after that.

She shakes her head at the memory. **SUZANNE** *gazes at the picture.*

LAURIE You were a cute baby.

SUZANNE *smiles.*

SUZANNE So were you. I didn't know you'd kept these, Mum.

ELEANOR Neither did I – I've found loads of funny old things, packing up the house. Like a secret gallery of my life.

A knock at the door. ELEANOR *is closest so she gets up and opens it, leaving* SUZANNE *and* LAURIE *looking at the picture.*

The room service WAITER *– same one as last time.*

Ah, here he is – come in, come in.

The WAITER *walks in with the three drinks on a tray. He is slightly wary.*

Tell me, young man – you are a young man, aren't you?

SUZANNE Mum...

WAITER Yes.

ELEANOR It's always good to check these days.

LAURIE Grandma, leave him alone.

ELEANOR Just a moment – tell me, young man, do you think my granddaughter is an attractive young woman?

The WAITER *looks at* LAURIE *a little bashfully.*

WAITER Uh, yes.

ELEANOR And would you prefer her in a dress? Perhaps with a more feminine haircut?

WAITER Uh, I think people should just wear whatever they want.

ELEANOR But don't we also send messages with what we wear? You are wearing a uniform, so you're not wearing whatever you want.

WAITER Well, I'm at work. I'd get sacked if I didn't wear it.

ELEANOR Exactly. Thank you.

She takes a gin and tonic off the tray, and sips it, looking triumphant.

SUZANNE I'm sorry about my mother. She's drunk.

ELEANOR I am not drunk.

SUZANNE Sorry – my mistake. She has "toothache". Let me
sign and then you can get out of here.

She signs. He looks grateful. He looks at LAURIE.

LAURIE Thanks.

WAITER You're very welcome.

He leaves swiftly.

LAURIE I can't believe you did that.

ELEANOR Did what? Just trying to get a little something going.
This is how you meet people – not through cold hard metal
and bunches of wires.

SUZANNE Just leave her to meet people however she chooses.
It's the way it works now. Stop trying to control everything.

ELEANOR Well it's all wrong. You have to smell the pheromones
on someone to know if you're a good fit. Then when you
mate you'll have healthy young.

LAURIE You make us sound like animals.

ELEANOR We are animals, darling. There's no getting away
from it. We are flesh and blood first and foremost.

LAURIE In the future, we're all gonna be part human, part robot.
Full humans will be extinct – a former dominant species,
exhibited in museums built by and for robots.

ELEANOR Will this be happening in the next twenty years or so?

LAURIE Oh, no…

ELEANOR Thank god for that – I'll be long dead.

LAURIE Not if we can keep you going with robotics.

ELEANOR Please don't. I wish to be powered by organic matter,
not petrol.

SUZANNE *(under her breath)* Could've fooled me.

ELEANOR You don't really want to be half robot, do you?

LAURIE Why not? I'll still be me, but a better version – stronger and healthier, more effective.

ELEANOR *and* **SUZANNE** *both consider this for a moment.*

SUZANNE I wouldn't mind having longer legs.

ELEANOR Yes, you got your father's legs.

SUZANNE What would you change, Mother? About yourself? If you could...

ELEANOR *thinks for a moment.*

ELEANOR I don't believe in trying to change ourselves – we are what we are.

SUZANNE *(to* **LAURIE***)* See? Told you.

ELEANOR Told her what?

SUZANNE That you won't analyse yourself, not even slightly. You're too scared.

ELEANOR Yes, scared of sitting around self-indulgently whingeing to an expensive stranger.

SUZANNE It's called therapy, Mother, I've found it to be very effective.

ELEANOR You've had therapy? Whatever for?

SUZANNE *cocks her head.*

Isn't it hugely expensive?

SUZANNE It's an investment.

ELEANOR In what?

SUZANNE Myself?

ELEANOR Well, what's the point of that?

SUZANNE *spreads her arms and almost laughs.*

Oh for goodness sake, I honestly don't know what's happened to the world – why did my grandmother march on the streets of London, risking a prison sentence to get women the vote, for equality? If she could see us now, she'd wonder if it was all worth the bother.

LAURIE I can vote this year. I'm grateful.

ELEANOR So you are still aware you are a "woman"?

LAURIE *(a bit like a mantra)* I don't believe in gender. Gender is a social construct.

ELEANOR You'd believe in it if you couldn't vote because of it, believe me.

LAURIE Yes, and so it's better to not have any gender restrictions at all. Or any gender.

ELEANOR But you believe we are born men and women, at least?

LAURIE No, I don't believe in biological sex, not in an either/ or way.

ELEANOR Well everyone I've met has been pretty either/or.

LAURIE But it's not as binary as that. It's more like a sliding scale. In the future, gender won't exist and neither will biological sex, at least not as we think of it. It'll just be individuals, billions of individuals with their own individual biological make-up.

ELEANOR What about babies? This is all very well, but you're going to have to make some babies at some point and then you'll find biological sex is more important than you think.

LAURIE There'll be external wombs to grow babies in. They've made one already. They'll mix the sperm and the egg in a tube, then transfer it to the artificial womb. Look...

She demonstrates this with empty glasses, the see-through plastic ice bucket, an olive from a pizza (slightly covered in tomato sauce) and a slurp of Prosecco. The final result is an olive floating in a lake of lightly pink Prosecco inside a transparent container, that sort of ends up looking like a cross-section of an early pregnancy in a plastic womb. LAURIE *plonks it down on the table and they all stop to look at it, unsure how to react.*

SUZANNE *watches all this agog, whilst eating cheese.*

ELEANOR And they say romance is dead – well I hope you'll still have dinner first.

LAURIE *gestures to the "womb" on the table.*

LAURIE You'll be able to look after it together – it'll be nice to share the responsibility so it's not all on the woman. You can have the womb in your house, it'll be made of glass or something so you can see each stage of the baby growing.

SUZANNE My god.

ELEANOR And how will you feed it? Sprinkle flakes from a tub onto the top of the amniotic fluid? Will you put a little ruined castle in the tank, for the baby to swim in and out of? Ridiculous.

As she speaks she mimes sprinkling fish food into the "womb". SUZANNE *goes over to the womb and pokes at the olive a bit, making it bob.*

SUZANNE So women won't even be having the babies in this future?

ELEANOR There you are, dear – your one achievement in life gone up in smoke.

SUZANNE That's sad.

LAURIE Why is it sad? Pregnancy and childbirth are the most dangerous things a woman can do.

SUZANNE Yes but even so, I loved carrying you, feeling you in there, singing to you, stroking you through my belly.

ELEANOR Don't say "belly". Horrible word.

LAURIE I can carry it, and stroke it. I can sing to it.

She picks it up and carries the womb around in front
her belly, pretending to stroke it, humming to it.

ELEANOR Oh god, put it down, it's revolting – although, at
least she can put it down!

LAURIE *grins and places it back on the table. She peers*
inside, almost as if she thinks it might move or grow. She
takes another olive off the remaining pizza and eats it.

SUZANNE Didn't you enjoy being pregnant, Mum? Or did you
hate having to give up drinking?

ELEANOR Well, actually you didn't have to back then. But no,
I can't honestly say I enjoyed being pregnant. I found it
frightening. And inconvenient.

LAURIE See? In the future, Grandma wouldn't have had to go
through any of it.

ELEANOR *(suddenly upset)* Then what's it all been for? What
did I give all up for? If I was born a hundred years later, my
life could have been totally different, is that it? No comfort
there.

SUZANNE If you'd been born a hundred years earlier your life
would have been totally different. You just play the hand
you're dealt.

ELEANOR But some are dealt easier hands than others. That's
the unfairness of it all.

SUZANNE It depends on how you view it.

ELEANOR Not true, not true – if I'd had the opportunities you've
had, I would have really made something of myself. I would
have achieved my potential. I had a spark – they all said I
had a spark. And it died, snuffed out, starved of oxygen in
the suffocating world of rules and expectations. That's why
I drank – haven't you worked it out? I was bored, I was so
fucking bored, at home with two kids, my life, my mind,
draining away before my very eyes.

So I drank to numb the panic and desperation. A hundred years earlier I'd have been put in a mental institution, like all the other clever women driven crazy by the boring mundanity of domestic life, with no way out.

SUZANNE *and* LAURIE *stare at* ELEANOR *as she recovers from this speech.*

SUZANNE *(genuine)* Would you like a drink?

ELEANOR *(automatic, slightly dazed)* Yes please, darling, you're a good girl.

SUZANNE And suddenly I'm twelve again.

She picks up the phone.

What shall I get?

ELEANOR A bottle of champagne. Good stuff. On me.

SUZANNE Really?

ELEANOR Yes, we should celebrate. We should. It's your special day.

SUZANNE *smiles – this was actually a nice flash of kindness from* ELEANOR *– it was unexpectedly sincere.*

SUZANNE A bottle of champagne please, in the Taylor Suite – yes, that one sounds good. Thank you.

She hangs up.

ELEANOR *looks around the room.*

ELEANOR I must say, it is a lovely suite. Gary's been very generous.

SUZANNE He is – he's a generous man.

ELEANOR Well that's a good quality to have in a husband. Your father was never stingy. He was careful, but never stingy.

SUZANNE I suppose Gary is a bit like Dad, in some ways.

LAURIE I don't really remember him – Grandad, I mean. I remember his smell though. Like pine.

ELEANOR Yes, he always smelt like a car freshener. His favourite aftershave. I couldn't get him to try another.

SUZANNE He was quite rigid.

ELEANOR He liked what he liked. He was consistent.

LAURIE Is that what you like about Gary, Mum?

SUZANNE Yes, that's one of the things I like – he's reliable.

LAURIE But don't you find it a bit boring?

SUZANNE Boring? God, no. There's nothing boring about a man who does what he says he's going to do. It's actually quite sexy.

LAURIE I'll take your word for it.

SUZANNE Just remember it, that's all. Once you get through shagging all the leather jackets, you may find a man in a sensible waterproof coat more appealing.

LAURIE You're saying my Dad was a leather jacket?

SUZANNE He was young. Maybe if we met again now, he'd be different. I know I'm different.

LAURIE (careful) Would you like to?

SUZANNE Like to what?

LAURIE Meet him now?

SUZANNE God, I don't know. There'd be so much to say, I'd end up saying none of it.

ELEANOR He wasn't good for you. He made you reckless.

SUZANNE Perhaps, perhaps that's true. But I felt very excited and alive.

ELEANOR That's just a euphemism for good sex.

LAURIE *and* SUZANNE *both laugh in surprise.* ELEANOR *looks alarmed then pleased with herself.*

Well I'm glad I entertain you. Where's that champagne?

A knock at the door.

Ah. Very good.

LAURIE If it's that guy again, can we all just leave him alone, please? He's trying to do his job without being harassed.

ELEANOR Quite right.

LAURIE *goes over to the door and opens it. She blocks the path of the* WAITER *so he doesn't come in, thereby protecting him from further scrutiny. He seems to be engaging her in conversation for a moment.* ELEANOR *and* SUZANNE *are straining to hear without being too obvious about it.* LAURIE *laughs suddenly and takes the bottle. The* WAITER *smiles and walks away down the corridor as she shuts the door.*

She takes the bottle over to the table. ELEANOR *and* SUZANNE *watch her, bursting to know what went on but not quite daring to ask.* LAURIE *seems oblivious, with just a private little smile on her face. She starts to open the bottle and then becomes aware of the eyes on her and looks up, slightly startled.*

LAURIE Jesus, what?!

SUZANNE What did he say, what did he say?

LAURIE *blushes a little.*

ELEANOR She's blushing, she's blushing – god, it's good to know some things haven't changed – women still blush, that's a bloody comfort.

SUZANNE What did he say?

LAURIE Nothing.

SUZANNE Didn't look like nothing. You laughed – what did he say? Was he flirting? You were flirting.

ELEANOR Alright dear, don't interrogate her – she has the right to a private life too, you know. *(Beat. Can't contain herself)* What did he say? Did he ask you out?

LAURIE Oh Grandma, no one asks each other out anymore.

ELEANOR Well what then?

LAURIE He asked me for my Instagram handle.

ELEANOR Your what?

SUZANNE It's a website with pictures – like an old-fashioned photo album online, but with more food.

ELEANOR Food?

SUZANNE Yes, food – you'll have heard it talked about. So you told him, then?

LAURIE Yeah.

SUZANNE And what made you laugh?

LAURIE *(smiling in spite of herself)* Oh god, I can't remember.

SUZANNE You can.

ELEANOR She can.

LAURIE Ok, he said, "If you can get past my white-cis-male-privilege, then I'd love to connect with you".

Silence.

ELEANOR I don't even understand what that means.

SUZANNE No...

LAURIE It's just a joke.

ELEANOR Is it a good joke?

LAURIE I laughed. It was quite bold of him, that's all. I could've been offended.

ELEANOR Why? Was it rude, what he said?

SUZANNE It's not a different language, Mum.

ELEANOR It feels like one.

> LAURIE's *phone buzzes. She looks at it, smiles to herself and then swipes her finger across.*

What was that? What are you doing? What's she doing?

LAURIE *(smiling coyly)* Nothing!

ELEANOR That was him, wasn't it? Bloody hell – already?

SUZANNE Did you swipe right on him?

> LAURIE *nods naughtily.* SUZANNE *claps her hands with glee.*

ELEANOR I am officially lost. I am still trying to work out the "joke".

LAURIE Don't worry about it, Grandma – honestly, it was just a stupid joke, like an ice-wrecker, or whatever you guys used to call it.

ELEANOR Ice-breaker. Don't you young ones need ice-breakers anymore? What do you do at parties?

LAURIE We all already know each other. We've all met online before we go.

> ELEANOR *looks around, appealing to some sort of invisible jury of her peers.*

> LAURIE *pours out glasses of champagne. She hands them out and raises hers. They are all a bit drunk by now.*

(giddy) To progress, to the individual, to defining your own destiny!

> *The other two are bit overwhelmed by this and drink mutely.* LAURIE *laughs and falls back on the sofa. She seems very happy all of a sudden.* SUZANNE *is a*

bit confused but also delighted. She sits down next to
LAURIE.

SUZANNE So lovely to see you laugh.

LAURIE Well, this is nice champagne. Come on, Grandma, come and sit with us too.

> **ELEANOR** *perches slightly stiffly.*

Come on, not like that – let's get close, like a family.

She pulls **ELEANOR** *to her, and also* **SUZANNE** *on the other side.* **SUZANNE** *leans in,* **ELEANOR** *sort of endures it, but she is also pleased in her way. They lie together, slumped into the couch, champagne glasses in hand and* **LAURIE** *with an arm around each one.* **LAURIE** *then takes out her phone and holds it at arm's length.*

LAURIE Selfie!

The three women smile for the camera as she takes the shot.

Pause.

Lights dim, music plays, actors move slowly to new positions.

Lights up. **ELEANOR** *is reclining on a chair on one side of the room, listening to music on* **LAURIE**'s *phone, using* **LAURIE**'s *headphones. She seems serene.* **SUZANNE** *and* **LAURIE** *sit together on the other side of the room, with* **SUZANNE** *in a chair and* **LAURIE** *at her feet on the floor. The scene is peaceful.*

LAURIE Tell me about when I was born, Mum.

SUZANNE Again?

LAURIE I like hearing it.

SUZANNE Well, it began late at night. I was at home – at Grandma and Grandad's I mean, and I wasn't due for another five days. Everyone said that your first will be late, so I thought I had at least a week left. I was so huge by that point, I barely got out of bed, but my dad would bring me sandwiches and biscuits.

LAURIE Where was Grandma?

SUZANNE Around, she was always around, but she wasn't very... practical.

LAURIE Was she...?

LAURIE *indicates* ELEANOR.

SUZANNE Drunk? Yes, probably. But she's right about one thing – she sort of kept it hidden. It was a lack of interest more than anything, punctuated by manic rages and long periods of lying down.

LAURIE So Grandad looked after you?

SUZANNE Mostly – he did his best.

LAURIE And where was my dad?

SUZANNE He'd gone by that point.

LAURIE Maybe he regrets it.

SUZANNE Well, no point in that – it only gives you cancer.

LAURIE I'm not sure that's scientific.

SUZANNE Maybe not, but science can't explain everything.

LAURIE But it can. It's just we don't know how to use it yet.

SUZANNE I like a bit of mystery. I don't know if I want everything explained. Can't we hold on to a little magic?

LAURIE Perhaps. Anyway, carry on.

SUZANNE So I started to feel the pains, deep pain, inside like a hot knife, then it would fall away for a bit, and then come again. Your grandad decided he didn't want to take any risks so he drove me to the hospital. She came, but she complained all the way. Said we were overreacting. We got into the hospital just as dawn was breaking. They wheeled me into the labour ward – Grandma and Grandad stayed out in the waiting room.

LAURIE So you were on your own?

SUZANNE Oh no, there were two wonderful midwives, with strong arms. And in the end, you didn't take long to come out – I was young, young and bendy, and not so full of fear as women are now. I just did as I was told and out you came.

LAURIE What did I look like?

SUZANNE They held you up, they said, "Don't panic if she doesn't cry straight away," but I heard you before I saw you. They raised you up from between my thighs, and you were covered in grey gunk, hair matted all over your head, and a huge lump of neon yellow snot coming out of your nose. And you were screaming, screaming, screaming, but not angry, it was almost like relief, like you were pleased to be out, out in the world, ready to get started. And that's how I always think of you – you couldn't wait to get started.

LAURIE *sighs contentedly and leans against her mother.* SUZANNE *kisses the top of her head.* ELEANOR *removes the headphones and is now quietly listening to* SUZANNE.

It's an incredible thing, you know, to knit a whole new person with your body. Don't wish it away too fast. There's power in it, as well as the danger, the trauma, there's power too. Fearsome, dark, wild power.

LAURIE *nods.*

LAURIE *sighs happily, but with a note of apprehension. We see her decide that this is a good moment...*

Mum...

SUZANNE Yes, love.

LAURIE I need to tell you something.

SUZANNE *(a bit wary now)* Are you pregnant?

LAURIE No, I'm not pregnant.

ELEANOR Course she's not, and even if she is, it's nothing to worry about because it's growing by itself in a wheelbarrow down the end of the garden. Just chuck a bit of compost on it from time to time.

She gestures to the ice bucket womb, still on the table.

LAURIE *is suddenly quite serious.* **SUZANNE** *sits up to look at her properly.*

SUZANNE Come on now, you're scaring me – out with it, quick.

LAURIE *takes a breath.*

LAURIE Promise not to be angry?

SUZANNE I can't promise anything until I know what it is...

LAURIE Please, just promise not to be angry.

SUZANNE Ok, ok, I promise, now tell me.

LAURIE I've seen my dad.

ELEANOR *gets up instantly, smooths her skirt and walks away from the sofa. She pours champagne into her glass.*

SUZANNE *is blindsided.*

SUZANNE *(whispered)* What? Where?

LAURIE At his house.

SUZANNE His house?

LAURIE Yes.

SUZANNE Where's his house?

LAURIE Berlin.

SUZANNE You went to Berlin? When?

SUZANNE *is having trouble processing this.* **LAURIE** *nods.*

LAURIE In August. I did it at the end of my inter-railing trip. It seemed...easy. Weirdly easy.

SUZANNE Why didn't you tell me before?

LAURIE I wanted time to process it myself.

SUZANNE How did you... How did you?

LAURIE Find him?

SUZANNE Yes.

LAURIE It's easy these days, if you really want to find someone, and they're not specifically hiding, you can find them.

SUZANNE But I looked. And I couldn't...

LAURIE Where?

SUZANNE Facebook.

LAURIE Oh he's not on Facebook.

ELEANOR Even I'm on Facebook.

LAURIE You have to go deeper than Facebook sometimes.

SUZANNE And you found him? And you went there? And met him?

LAURIE Yes. He asked about you – wanted to know all about how you are. He's... He's really nice. And... And I got you this.

She pulls a piece of folded paper out of her pocket. She holds it out. SUZANNE *looks at it but doesn't take it.*

SUZANNE What's that?

LAURIE A ticket. A plane ticket to Berlin. I got it for you. I printed it out and everything. I wanted it to feel real. I wanted you to see him.

SUZANNE *breathes out and slumps back like a deflated balloon, leaving* LAURIE *holding the piece of paper awkwardly. Her arm drops to her side. She is uncertain of her herself now.*

Mum? Are you ok?

SUZANNE *says nothing – just stares at the floor.* LAURIE *looks to* ELEANOR *for reassurance.*

Grandma?

ELEANOR Not a hundred per cent sure you should've done all that tonight, dear.

LAURIE *looks back at her mother, who seems to be in a bit of a daze. She is beginning to feel she has made a mistake.*

LAURIE Mum?

LAURIE *shakes her arm a bit, a little alarmed.*

MUM!

SUZANNE *sits up and appears to pull herself together.*

SUZANNE Yes, sorry. So, you met your dad. I think that's wonderful. I'm so glad you got on. Is it a bit hot in here? Does the window open, I wonder? They don't usually, do they, in hotels, in case people try to jump out, I should think. Looks bad for a nice hotel, doesn't it, with bodies all over the pavement outside reception. I am starving – is anyone else hungry?

She gets up.

Where's the menu. I could eat, suddenly – god, must be all the booze.

LAURIE Is that it?

SUZANNE *studies the menu.*

SUZANNE Is that what?

LAURIE Is that all you're going to say about it?

SUZANNE Yes, I should think so. You've told me now, and I said I was pleased, so you can stop worrying about it.

LAURIE But how do you feel about...

SUZANNE Don't interrogate me, darling. I said that's enough.

LAURIE Jesus, you sound just like her.

She gestures to ELEANOR.

I thought you were supposed to be in touch with your feelings?

SUZANNE I am in touch with my feelings. The ones I like, anyway, and I think I'd like a burger. That's the feeling I'm most in touch with now. Something big and greasy and dirty. Shall we all have one?

ELEANOR You're sounding a bit...panicked, darling.

SUZANNE Because of a burger? Well maybe that's panicking to you, Mother, but to most people eating burgers is perfectly normal. Laurie, do you want one?

LAURIE No... Mum...

SUZANNE Come on, Mother – you need to eat something.

ELEANOR Do they do sushi?

SUZANNE *(bit sarcastic, pretending to look, barely under control)* Do they do sushi, do they do sushi, let's see now, sushi, sushi, sushi – nope, sorry, Mother, you're out of luck there. Shall I just order you an empty plate and a knife and fork instead?

SUZANNE *picks up the phone to order.*

ELEANOR Thank you, dear.

SUZANNE *(into the phone)* Hello, yes, Taylor Suite again, yes, a burger please, everything on it, everything on the side. Thank you. Thank you very much.

She slams the phone down a bit too hard.

LAURIE MUM!

SUZANNE WHAT?

LAURIE *looks exasperated.*

What do you want me to say to you, Lauren? What? You found your dad, good for you. You saw him, good for you. You got on, good for you. What else? What else should I say? Should I ask you where he lives so I can run over there and he can ask me to marry him, and suddenly the last eighteen years will vanish and everything will be perfect and we will live happily ever after? Is that what you had in mind?

LAURIE I just wanted to see you together, just once – is that too much to ask? Maybe you'd remember how you felt back then...

ELEANOR *shakes her head.* **LAURIE** *brushes a tear away angrily.*

SUZANNE Grow up! Listen, I'm sorry, but I can't provide whatever perfect vision you've got in your head. I don't even know the man. I don't even know him. He fucked me, and then he fucked off. That was half a lifetime ago. He doesn't know me. I don't know him. We are strangers. And you know who's not a stranger? Gary, that's who. Gary, who I am marrying tomorrow. Good, kind, generous, dependable Gary, and maybe then I will have a chance at some kind of normal, adult life, and I can stop worrying about the mountain of debt I can barely breathe under.

She stops – she didn't mean to say that. **LAURIE** *and* **ELEANOR** *are looking at her intently as she recovers her breath. For a moment, Christian is forgotten.*

LAURIE What mountain of debt?

SUZANNE Forget I said it.

ELEANOR How much debt are you in, exactly?

SUZANNE Am I invisible? Has everyone suddenly gone deaf? I said forget about it. It's my problem and I'm dealing with it. With Gary's help.

ELEANOR I see, I see, I see. Now all becomes clear.

SUZANNE What exactly becomes clear?

ELEANOR Suzanne, how much debt are you in?

SUZANNE It's under control.

ELEANOR Ten thousand? Twenty?

SUZANNE Please stop.

ELEANOR Fifty? A hundred?

> SUZANNE *looks away.*

> A hundred thousand pounds? Tell me it's less than a hundred thousand pounds.

> SUZANNE *looks straight at her, defiantly.*

SUZANNE It's less than a hundred thousand pounds.

She holds her gaze.

ELEANOR *(steely)* How. Much. Less?

SUZANNE I am a grown woman, I have a right to privacy. I have never asked you for anything. I am sorting it out. Now I mean it – leave me alone.

ELEANOR And I suppose my right to privacy was waived when you found that letter from the school and decided to broadcast its contents to my granddaughter earlier this evening?

SUZANNE That's different.

ELEANOR How is it different?

SUZANNE Because you have blamed me and Dad and John your whole life for your failures, and we believed you, and it turned out you were lying, and it was your fault all along. That's why. I, on the other hand, blame no one but myself.

LAURIE I thought you had money for things. For my accommodation. You just paid it.

SUZANNE Credit cards, my love, all credit cards. But it's ok – you've not to worry – Gary is sorting it out.

ELEANOR So you haven't got it under control.

SUZANNE Mum, I said leave it. Can you, for once in your life, respect me enough to do as I ask and LEAVE ME ALONE?

ELEANOR For god's sake, darling, everyone needs a good accountant from time to time, but you don't have to marry him.

SUZANNE, without warning, slaps ELEANOR. ELEANOR gasps and then slaps her back. SUZANNE grabs the womb ice bucket, lifts it above her head, and makes to throw the contents at ELEANOR. ELEANOR ducks. LAURIE lunges to stop her.

LAURIE MUM! NO!

She grabs at the womb ice bucket, and manages to get her hands round it, gently take it from her mother, and set it down on the table again. She looks at it for a moment, almost as if she really has rescued a pregnancy. She stands in front of it, guarding it, taking a breath.

She wheels round to her mother and grandmother.

Just stop it, both of you!

They stand quietly, clutching their cheeks that sting.

What the hell is going on tonight? What the hell is going on? We're meant to be having a lovely family evening of bonding before Mum's wedding.

ELEANOR Well you'd better find some other family to have it with, because it's not happening here.

SUZANNE She came in with an attitude, and I'm am simply reacting.

ELEANOR I came in no different to how I always come in.

SUZANNE Exactly. EXACTLY. Just admit it, you can't stand to
see me happy, so you have to try and ruin it. You can't stand
to see that a man loves me, even though I may be a mess.

ELEANOR How can you say this? What a thing to accuse me
of – you're my daughter, of course I want you to be happy.

SUZANNE Then show me – don't just make shitty, snide little
remarks about my dress, or my underwear, or what food I'm
going to eat, or what colour rose Gary gets for you. Be nice.
Would it fucking kill you to be nice? Just straightforwardly
nice, without all the fucking backstory.

ELEANOR I am entitled to an opinion about my own daughter
and how she chooses to live her life. I love you.

SUZANNE Do you?

ELEANOR Oh Suzanne, just because someone doesn't endlessly
babble on about their feelings, doesn't mean...

SUZANNE Have you ever heard the term "emotionally absent"?

ELEANOR No, and I'm glad I haven't. Is this something your
therapist has made up to get more money out of you?

SUZANNE You never wanted to spend time with me. It was like
you didn't even want to be around me.

ELEANOR *(careless, provoked)* Well you got on my nerves.

LAURIE *gasps.* SUZANNE *glances at her.*

SUZANNE You see? *(to* ELEANOR*)* You always preferred John
anyway.

ELEANOR Well John didn't make such a bloody fuss about
everything all the time. You were completely impossible – I
don't know how any mother would have coped with your
endless demands, and phobias, and particular little ways.
I remember one summer I had to literally *hold a change of
clothes for you in my hand* at all times, at your little-madame
insistence, because you wanted to play in the garden but

went berserk if you got the tiniest speck of dirt on your skirt. I mean, I ask you...

She appeals to LAURIE *who shrugs awkwardly.*

SUZANNE Did it ever occur to you I wanted a bit of attention?

ELEANOR Did it ever occur to you that I didn't have anything left to give you?

SUZANNE I give up. I fucking give up. You win – you were the perfect mother, and I, as always, am the mess. The end.

ELEANOR Do you think I had a perfect mother? Do you think anyone has? Do you think Laurie has a perfect mother?

LAURIE Don't bring me into this.

They both swing to look at LAURIE, *who, caught in the glare, sees she needs to respond to make it stop, although she is still smarting about the plane ticket.*

I don't know what I'm supposed to say. You did your best.

SUZANNE See?

ELEANOR I think that's a nice way of saying you were a mess. A well-meaning mess, but a mess all the same.

SUZANNE *sits down heavily and starts crying.* ELEANOR, *shocked, does not know what to do.*

LAURIE *instinctively goes to her and puts her arms around her mother.*

LAURIE Are you ok, Mum?

SUZANNE *wipes her eyes.*

SUZANNE Thanks love, I'm ok, I'm ok, you're a good girl.

ELEANOR *goes to pour herself a drink. She fills her glass and downs it.*

LAURIE *and* SUZANNE *hug tightly.* ELEANOR *is alone on the other side of the room, observing them.*

It's ok, it's ok. I'm getting married in the morning. Everything is going to get sorted out. And you're doing brilliantly at university and that makes me very happy.

LAURIE I know it's a good thing – Gary's a good guy, I'm not saying he isn't. But love is important too, isn't it?

ELEANOR *(trying to make light)* Won't all this seem a bit wafty when the robots come?

SUZANNE *(snaps)* Leave her alone.

ELEANOR *is slightly taken aback – the tone was harsher than expected.*

LAURIE *(turning to* ELEANOR *with passion, unbowed)* I believe in love. They're not mutually exclusive – one day, even robots will be capable of love.

ELEANOR Of course they won't. Robots can't do that – love is a human response.

SUZANNE Which seems to have passed you by.

ELEANOR *(frustration)* FOR GOD'S SAKE, SUZANNE, WHY CAN'T YOU SEE? I LOVE YOU, I AM JUST DISAPPOINTED IN YOU. I am disappointed for you because I can see what you could have been.

SUZANNE No, you see what you could've been. I couldn't have been any of those things you wanted. I was average, just very average. And I have learnt to accept that about myself, through lots of talking, and yes, therapy. I have learnt to accept that I don't have to be what you wanted to be yourself in order to be happy. I am not going to be famous, or rich, or successful. I am going to be a married forty-year-old woman who lives in Hitchin with a good man and a wonderful daughter. There is nothing wrong with that. Nothing wrong with ME. Your self-loathing is not my problem anymore. I push it away.

She stands up and makes a pushing away gesture.

ELEANOR What on earth was that?

SUZANNE *pushes again.*

SUZANNE I push it away.

ELEANOR You did it again. She did it again.

SUZANNE *pushes again, harder now, right up to* ELEANOR.

SUZANNE I push it away.

ELEANOR What are you doing now? What's she doing?

SUZANNE I am visualising something damaging to me, and then physically pushing it away.

ELEANOR *has not moved at all in this time.* SUZANNE *has closed her eyes and is drawing a slow circle around her head with her finger, while breathing deeply.*

ELEANOR *observes.*

ELEANOR What's that?

LAURIE A circle of protection.

ELEANOR Don't tell me you're into this as well?

LAURIE Not really my thing, but you know, we're all different – whatever works.

ELEANOR *(to* SUZANNE*)* Is this something you learnt on one of these weekend retreats you insist on going on?

SUZANNE Yes, it is, and it really helps.

She continues with the circle drawing.

ELEANOR You might as well put an ash cross on your door when you see me coming.

SUZANNE Believe me, I've tried.

SUZANNE *breathes out, puts her arms by her sides and opens her eyes. She does seem calmer and more centred. Now* ELEANOR *seems deflated. She also sinks to a chair.*

ELEANOR Do you really hate me this much?

SUZANNE I don't know. I don't know if it's anger or hate. It's hard to tell the difference sometimes.

ELEANOR *nods. She seems smaller. There is a long silence.*

ELEANOR I'm sorry.

SUZANNE *looks up. She can't believe her ears. There is a pause.*

SUZANNE What was that?

ELEANOR You heard. Don't make me say it again.

SUZANNE Say it again. You can manage once more.

ELEANOR *(with difficultly, clearing her throat first)* I'm sorry.

SUZANNE Sorry for what?

LAURIE Mum, don't.

SUZANNE Please – I've waited forty years to hear this.

ELEANOR *bows her head.*

And the drinking? And the rages? And the constant drip-drip of blame?

ELEANOR *seems to shrink further.*

ELEANOR Yes, I'm sorry for all of it.

SUZANNE And you admit you had – have – a drinking problem?

LAURIE Mum, this feels cruel.

SUZANNE It may feel cruel, Laurie, but it's important. It really is.

ELEANOR I admit I...could've handled the drinking...better.

SUZANNE And it was a problem. For the family. It made a problem.

ELEANOR I can see that it was difficult for you.

SUZANNE Problem, say "problem".

ELEANOR Please, Suzanne, that's all I can manage for now. Please.

SUZANNE *pauses, and then nods. There is a long silence while they all take stock. Then* SUZANNE *nods.*

SUZANNE Ok, ok – that'll do. That's enough. You can go freely and drink yourself to death in Italy now. I won't bring it up again.

ELEANOR *(whispered)* Thank you.

ELEANOR *leans her head against the chair wing.*

SUZANNE Now, I really want that burger.

LAURIE *is mute. She is shocked. She stares at her mother.*

LAURIE I didn't know... I didn't know you had it in you.

SUZANNE *shrugs.*

SUZANNE I don't want to carry it around anymore.

They glance at ELEANOR *who has fallen asleep, her glass slipping in her hand.*

SUZANNE *walks over to* ELEANOR *and gently removes the glass from her hand and sets it on the table. She then even more gently pushes her mother's head back into the chair because it had slumped forward at an awkward angle.*

LAURIE You did that without waking her.

SUZANNE Oh sweetie, I must've done that a thousand times in my life. She always sleeps when she doesn't like something. It's quite a skill.

LAURIE *nods.*

SUZANNE Can I give you a bit of advice before I become an old married woman?

LAURIE Ok...

SUZANNE Don't ever just do things because you feel you ought to. Prioritise your own happiness, your own dreams, your own *life*. You can suffocate under the weight of all the duty and expectation. Throw it all off and just do what you want. Don't be cruel with it, but just be happy. It seems like sometimes, people don't want to be responsible for their own happiness – it's like they'd almost rather be miserable, and then say, "But it's not my fault". Don't do that, Laurie, promise me – you're allowed to be happy, so chase your own happiness. Promise me.

LAURIE Ok. I will.

SUZANNE Good. Good.

LAURIE And what about you? Can you make me the same promise?

SUZANNE Yes. I will try.

LAURIE Did... Did I...

SUZANNE Did you what?

LAURIE Did I hold you back?

SUZANNE No! My god, no. You never held me back from anything. The only thing that held me back was me.

LAURIE What would make you happy?

SUZANNE I just want to give in, now. That's what I want. All my life I've been told I'm supposed to be achieving some nameless goal, and I don't know what it is and no one can tell me, it's just meant to be "more".

But I don't want more – I just want to be married to Gary, boring old Gary, and live in a nice house in Hitchin with no debt, and a little shop down the road, and a favourite pub in town, the odd nice meal out, and a holiday somewhere hot in January every year, if I'm lucky. That's it. I'm tired of aspiring. I want to settle. I want to be average. That's my dirty secret. That's my dirty, shameful secret.

LAURIE It's ok, Mum, it's ok. It sounds nice.

LAURIE *hugs* SUZANNE. SUZANNE *rests her head against* LAURIE*'s chest, and* LAURIE *cradles her mother for a moment as if* SUZANNE *is the child. They stay quiet like this for a moment then* SUZANNE *yawns deeply, as if she is suddenly tired from years of effort.*

She nestles on LAURIE *and also falls asleep.* LAURIE *takes her glass out of her hand before it falls and puts it on the side table. She looks from one to the other and shakes her head, shell-shocked from it all.*

There is a soft knock at the door. Neither ELEANOR *nor* SUZANNE *stirs.* LAURIE *disentangles herself from her mother and goes to answer it. It is the* WAITER, *holding a tray groaning under the weight of the burger with all its side orders.*

LAURIE *puts her finger to her lips and motions him to come in. He looks at the two sleeping women, and all the empty bottles of booze and smirks at* LAURIE. *She smiles back.*

He goes to the table. He sees the ice bucket womb, starts slightly, and then picks it up carefully, very carefully so as not to spill it, and moves it to a higher side table. LAURIE *watches him do this with an almost tender expression on her face.*

He then puts the burger tray down carefully and quietly, where the ice bucket womb was. LAURIE *signs for the food, and they hold the bill wallet together for a moment. They look straight into each other's eyes.*

WAITER You swiped right on me.

LAURIE You swiped right on me first...

They smile at it other, holding the moment. Then she drops the bill wallet and leans in to kiss him. He hesitates and then kisses her back. They kiss passionately for a moment, starting to touch each other.

(NB at this point the following action can take place slightly offstage, out of full view of the audience)

They sink down, getting more into it. He moves down her body. He stops.

WAITER Are you sure?

LAURIE *glances at the sleeping women, nods and he continues.* **SUZANNE** *shifts a bit. They both freeze. She is still asleep, snoring ever so slightly.*

They giggle quietly and he moves his head down towards the area between her legs. **LAURIE** *tries to keep her breathing under control. She pulls a large cushion on to her lap to try and cover what's going on. She is breathing more heavily now and closes her eyes a little, head tipped back.*

She tips her head straight again, briefly opens her eyes, and stares straight into the open eyes of **ELEANOR**, *who has woken up but not moved a muscle, and has been watching.* **LAURIE** *jumps.* **ELEANOR** *snaps her eyes shut again, pretending to be asleep.*

LAURIE *(whispers)* Shit. Ok, ok...

She gently but urgently pulls the **WAITER**'s *head up from under her skirt.*

WAITER *(whispers)* What? No good? People say I'm good.

LAURIE It was wonderful but you've got to go now.

WAITER Don't get me sacked.

She jostles him to the door.

LAURIE No, no – of course not, no, no. I'll message you. Thanks for the burger.

WAITER Likewise.

LAURIE What?

WAITER Nothing. Confused. Ok, thanks, ok. Shit.

LAURIE *shoves him out the door and closes it. She pauses for a moment and then turns to face her grandma who is now sitting up primly, legs crossed, and grinning widely, trying not to laugh.*

ELEANOR Your grandfather never did that to me.

LAURIE Well, maybe he should've.

ELEANOR Yes, maybe he should've.

SUZANNE *is stirring now. They both look at her, slightly alarmed.*

LAURIE Grandma – please...don't say...

ELEANOR *shakes her head and puts her finger to her lips. Her eyes gleam with amusement though.*

SUZANNE *sits up and rubs her eyes.*

SUZANNE I can smell chips. Burger and chips.

They all look at the food. They are all suddenly starving.

SUZANNE *grabs at the burger and takes a big bite.*

Oh god, there it is. Better than sex.

ELEANOR *smirks at* LAURIE. LAURIE *blushes.*

Want some?

She offers the burger to **LAURIE**. **LAURIE** *takes it and bites into it.*

LAURIE I'm meant to be a vegan this month.

SUZANNE Do it next month instead.

LAURIE *nods, mouth full of burger.*

Come on, Mum – you've got to be hungry by now.

She thrusts the dripping, cheese covered burger at her mother. **ELEANOR** *gets a whiff of the smell and almost faints from hunger.*

ELEANOR Oh fuck it.

She also takes it and bites, they all chew now, happily.

And another.

She bites again.

Are there any chips?

SUZANNE I should think there are, yes. Chips! She wants chips! Yes, here we are, chips for all!

She reveals a plate of chips and they all dig in. **SUZANNE** *starts laughing, and becomes a little hysterical.*

ELEANOR *(mouth full)* What on earth is the matter?

SUZANNE You used to do this – nothing to eat all day, fall asleep pissed, wake up in the night and demolish the fridge and deny it all in the morning. "Lasagne? What lasagne?" – you practically still had the bechamel sauce dried to your chin!

ELEANOR Don't be ridiculous – that maybe happened twice. Three times at most during periods of high stress.

SUZANNE *is still laughing.*

SUZANNE I've just never actually seen you do it before, like in front of...people...witnesses. I feel like David Attenborough getting rare footage for the first time.

ELEANOR Well, Italy's changed me.

SUZANNE I'll say it has! All that grilled fish, eh? "No pasta of course."

She continues laughing. ELEANOR *rolls her eyes. She puts the plate with the chips and onion rings and remaining bits of burger between the three of them on the floor and they all crouch around it, eating with gusto, with their hands, licking their fingers. They are almost animal-like, in their own ways. It is like some kind of primitive shared feast. (Not too far with this – just a light suggestion of it.)*

They stop, satiated and each lie back onto a different comfortable sofa or chair.

ELEANOR What's the time?

SUZANNE No idea, but it's light.

She gestures to the window.

ELEANOR You're getting married in a few hours.

SUZANNE I am.

ELEANOR On my wedding day, I was up before dawn, with cucumbers on my face and a girdle to negotiate.

SUZANNE Poor you. Was it all worth it? For him?

ELEANOR I never hated your father, if that's what you were getting at.

SUZANNE But you weren't happy – why didn't you just leave?

ELEANOR I didn't know I could.

SUZANNE I assume you've got someone in Italy?

ELEANOR Well, I...

SUZANNE Don't be coy – what's his name?

ELEANOR Giulio.

SUZANNE And is he good to you? In bed I mean?

> ELEANOR *manufactures shock for a moment, and then glances at* LAURIE *briefly, who raises her eyebrows.*

Come on – that was always the problem, wasn't it? So?

ELEANOR Well, as a matter of fact, yes, since you ask – some very new...experiences. I feel like a different person out there. I am a different person out there.

> *They regard each other, woman to woman.* SUZANNE *nods.*

SUZANNE That is genuinely wonderful to hear.

ELEANOR Maybe you'll visit me sometime.

SUZANNE Maybe I will.

> *A pause.*

I think I'm going to get ready now. It won't take long. There'll be guests to meet soon. And I need to check the flowers.

> *The other two nod in agreement.* SUZANNE *takes her dress and goes into her bedroom and shuts the door, leaving* LAURIE *and* ELEANOR *together.*

LAURIE Shall I make some coffee?

ELEANOR That sounds like a good idea.

> LAURIE *finds the coffee making equipment and begins to make it.* ELEANOR *goes to the window and looks out. Dawn is beginning to break.*

> LAURIE *brings over a cup of coffee and hands it to her grandmother. She has one for herself too.*

Thank you, dear.

LAURIE No problem.

LAURIE*'s phone pings. She looks at it and smiles.*

ELEANOR Bit early for messages, isn't it?

LAURIE It's Rufus, the uh... The room service guy.

ELEANOR I see.

LAURIE He's finished his shift and wants to hook up.

ELEANOR What, now?

LAURIE Yeah.

ELEANOR Are you going to?

LAURIE I might find him later. Get a cup of tea or something.

ELEANOR Like an actual cup of tea?

LAURIE An actual cup of tea. I am still a human – I do need to imbibe liquid.

Pause.

ELEANOR You've heard a lot of things tonight. Shocking things, maybe. I hope... I hope you don't think less of your mother.

LAURIE God, no.

ELEANOR Or... Or me...

LAURIE No, I just think it's...sad.

ELEANOR Oh, no pity, please. I can't stand pity.

LAURIE I wish you'd had the life you wanted, or you felt you deserved.

ELEANOR I wasn't brave enough to do anything different.

LAURIE But you shouldn't have to be brave, that's my point. It shouldn't be an act of courage to have the life you want. It should be normal. It should be easy.

ELEANOR I hope that's true for you.

LAURIE Perhaps it will be. Perhaps the robots won't see gender at all. Maybe they will save us with their rational, non-gendered, biologically neutral status and we can start again, wipe the slate clean.

ELEANOR That's an old phrase – wipe the slate clean.

LAURIE Then you know what I'm talking about.

ELEANOR *nods.*

The bedroom door opens, and SUZANNE *enters in the wedding dress we saw earlier. It suits her. She looks genuinely lovely.*

Oh Mum – Oh mum – you look beautiful, just really beautiful.

SUZANNE Thanks, love. I feel like shit. Amazing what a kilo of make-up can do.

LAURIE Nah, you look great. Ok, my turn.

LAURIE *leaves to go to her bedroom and get ready.*

ELEANOR You can't beat a good night's sleep.

SUZANNE That wasn't ever going to happen.

ELEANOR No. Give us a twirl, then.

SUZANNE *does a twirl and the light fabric spins with her, fanning out. She looks almost girlish. It floats about her, softly settling.*

ELEANOR It's a lovely fabric, yes. And...it suits you. You look lovely, Suzanne. Very...comfortable.

It's stiff, but it's the best she can do. SUZANNE *knows it.*

SUZANNE Thanks, Mum.

They look at each other, and there is sort of a smile, or at least a type of new understanding.

ELEANOR Let me go and put my outfit on, then.

She goes into her bedroom, leaving **SUZANNE** *alone in the room. She pulls back the curtains, letting the morning light in. She catches her reflection in the window and twirls again. She smiles.*

She gathers up the three roses, red, white and yellow, and looks around. She sees what she is looking for, and pulls at a ribbon that is wrapped around one of the vases. She ties the three roses together, to become a bouquet. She smells them and smiles again.

LAURIE *re-enters, wearing her customised "men's" suit.*

SUZANNE Wow, don't you look handsome. *(Beat)* Laurie, did I do the wrong thing...with your dad?

LAURIE I don't know. I'm pleased I've seen him. I wish I'd done it sooner though.

SUZANNE Listen – that ticket – take it for yourself, ok? Change the name, or...or I'll even buy you a new one. Whatever, but spend some time with him. He'll like you. You'll like him.

LAURIE *nods.*

ELEANOR *also comes out of her bedroom wearing an elegant and perfectly fitting peach skirt suit, with matching heels, and a feather fascinator in her hair. The three of them couldn't look more different.*

SUZANNE You look lovely, Mum.

ELEANOR Thank you, dear. Look at the three of us.

They nod and look at each other for a moment. There is still a slight wariness in the room – all is not perfect, but they can now see each other in a different light.

SUZANNE Ready?

LAURIE Ready.

ELEANOR *nods too.*

SUZANNE Come on, then. *(A glint in her eye)* Let's go and make an honest woman of me.

They smile, and all leave the room, one by one, shutting the door behind them.

Lights out, with only the ice bucket womb illuminated on the table, just for a split second.

Blackout.

THIS
IS
NOT
THE
END

Lightning Source UK Ltd.
Milton Keynes UK
UKHW020424080921
390191UK00005B/266

9 780573 115585